An Introduction to Office Management for Secretaries

Also available from Cassell:

Effective Communication Skills Chris Simons

The Professional Secretary John Spencer and Adrian Pruss
Volume I: Communication Skills
Volume II: Management Skills

Informative Writing: Your Practical Guide to Effective Communication
Ken Goddard

An Introduction to Office Management for Secretaries

Désirée Cox
Illustrated by Peter Watkins

Cassell
Wellington House
125 Strand
London WC2R 0BB

PO Box 605
Herndon
VA 20172

© Désirée Cox 1998

All rights reserved. No part of this publication may be reproduced or transmitted in any form or by any means, electronic or mechanical including photocopying, recording or any information storage or retrieval system, without prior permission in writing from the publishers.

First published 1997

British Library Cataloguing-in-Publication Data
A catalogue record for this book is available from the British Library.

ISBN 0-304-70071-1 (hardback)
      0-304-70072-X (paperback)

Typeset by Fakenham Photosetting Limited, Fakenham, Norfolk
Printed and bound in Great Britain by Redwood Books, Trowbridge, Wiltshire

Contents

Acknowledgements	viii
Note	viii
Introduction	ix
Perception Awareness	1
Communicating with other people	3
Listening	3
Verbal communication	4
Body language	5
Appearance and attitude	15
Self-management	18
Making the best use of your time	18
Handling workload pressure	21
Organizing your working environment	22
Developing your working strategy	26
The Professional Approach	29
Projects	30
Customer care	35
Quality standards	37
Working with People	39
Your manager	39
Working in a departmental or project team	40
Working in a secretarial team	42
Working with other departments	43
Communication	44
Telephone communication	44
Answerphones and voicemail systems	47
Facsimile transmissions	47
Written communication	48
Office Practice	55
Handling mail	55
Bring forward file	56
Record maintenance	57

Contents

    Signature book   58
    Filing   59

Diaries and Travel   61
    Diary control   61
    Travel arrangements   63

Meetings and Events   66
    Teleconferencing   66
    Videoconferencing   66
    Scheduling a meeting   68
    Presentations   70
    Organizing events   72

Information Technology in the Office   76
    What is a computer?   76
    Different types of computer   77
    How a computer works   79
    Input devices   80
    Output devices   82
    Printers   82
    Storage   84
    Networks   86
    Electronic communication   88
    Security   90
    The Computer Misuse Act   90
    The Data Protection Act   91
    What is software?   91
    Word processing   92
    Spreadsheets   93
    Databases   94
    Presentation packages   95
    Desktop publishing   96
    Acronyms, abbreviations and terminology   97

Simple Accounting   98
    Glossary of accounting terms   99
    Assets and liabilities   99
    The balance sheet   100
    Profit and loss accounts (P&L)   101
    Petty cash   103
    Budgets   105
    Expenses   106
    Purchasing   107
    Payment of invoices   108

Business and Organization	109
The public sector: structure and control	109
The private sector: business ownership	110
Organization structure	112
Roles and responsibilities	113
Sales	114
Marketing	116
Personnel	118
Finance	119
Administration	120
Appendix 1: Useful Telephone Numbers	122
Railway telephone information services	122
World airlines telephone information services	123
Regional airport telephone numbers	123
UK hotel group telephone information services	124
Car hire companies: central reservation numbers	124
Other useful numbers	124
Appendix 2: Secretarial Survey	126
The survey	126
Results	127
Index	129

Acknowledgements

I would like to thank all those who contributed to this book in some way. In particular my thanks go to: my parents, for their advice and suggestions on input; Caroline Wren for her prompt proofreading, editing and correcting; Peter Watkins for his illustrations on body language; and finally my husband, Vincent, for the material he provided for several of the chapters, and more importantly for his support and enthusiasm.

Note

For the sake of simplicity, I have referred to the secretary as 'she' and the manager as 'he' throughout the book. This in no way indicates that secretaries are always female, or that managers are always male.

Introduction

The role of the secretary has expanded dramatically over the past 20 years as the technological revolution has made its impact on the office environment.

With the advent of the electronic office and the changes it brings, today's secretary needs to be a centre of competence in technology. This is particularly true as computers invade the office and baffle many of the more senior managers, who in turn rely upon their secretaries to keep their offices running smoothly without exposing them to the vagaries of the electronic world. Traditional duties have become enhanced, the job has developed into a key role in the organization and the secretary now holds a valuable position – an essential piece of the corporate jigsaw.

The word 'secretary' is derived from 'secret', meaning 'keeper of the secrets'. This old-fashioned value hasn't changed: a secretary is still expected to be discreet and loyal to the boss, yet more and more bosses will listen to and value the opinions of their secretaries.

In the past, the secretarial profession has often been criticized for its incompetence and ineffectiveness. Secretaries were seen as spinster dragons or blonde bimbos. Fortunately, today the profession has gained a healthier reputation – secretaries are respected for their skills and their professionalism. It is no longer such a female-dominated environment, with a growing proportion of male secretaries being accepted in the workplace.

Women started to appear in offices in the 1930s, when they were employed to operate machinery such as typewriters. The Second World War contributed to the explosion of female office workers and slowly they became a fixed asset in every organization. Historically, people drifted into secretarial work after studying basic shorthand and typing, often beginning in the typing pool and progressing from junior to senior secretary, then to personal assistant. For many it was through lack of opportunities in the workplace; for others it was a stopgap between school and marriage. There were certainly no opportunities for advancement beyond the limited secretarial world.

Today young people are more ambitious, looking for a career and not just a job. Those who join the secretarial ranks are frequently seeking a fulfilling and rewarding career.

A secretarial career has much to offer. It can be a very self-satisfying role, or a stepping stone to gain extensive knowledge of an organization before moving into a different area. It is a logical starting point for those seeking a career in administration, communications or public relations.

Yet the role has become a much more demanding one. A secretary today is expected not only to be competent, but to excel in all areas – understanding all aspects of the job and being the centre of proficiency in the workplace.

A survey conducted of the top 50 companies in the UK, together with a selection of financial institutions and secretarial colleges, has shown that today's employers are seeking to recruit secretaries of a different calibre. They are looking for people who possess superb secretarial credentials, embrace electronic technology with enthusiasm and combine this with excellent personal skills. More and more companies are realizing that secretaries need to be more than an extension of the typewriter. Computer literacy and knowledge of various systems is vital to compete in today's electronic office. Yet, equally, companies are seeking flexible people with a positive attitude who will play an active role in the organization.

Employers are beginning to realize that the secretary is frequently the first contact a company will have with its customers; therefore she needs to be intelligent, capable and well informed. A secretary is the bridge between a business and its customers, and is the vital link with the outside world.

Customer care and customer satisfaction often depend upon this first contact and it is therefore a very important and privileged position. Someone recently said to me that a secretary must be one of the most important employees in an organization, because when a director or senior manager leaves it is often several weeks or months before he is replaced, but when a secretary leaves she has to be replaced immediately because without her the business cannot function. This is very true and really shows how valuable an asset a secretary is to a company.

This book is not a secretarial manual. Although it looks briefly at the traditional processes still performed by secretaries today and various ways to make these easier, it is primarily concerned with adding value (and interest) by combining personal skills with business proficiency. It is aimed at those secretaries looking to enhance their current skills, to develop their potential and to find satisfaction in a professional secretarial role.

My personal hope is that it will encourage people to seek fulfilment and enjoyment from their role – being a secretary is probably one of the most privileged positions in an organization and should never be underestimated.

Perception Awareness

Perception awareness is all about how you see others and how they see you. It is influenced by several different factors:

- the five senses of touch, sight, hearing, taste and smelling;
- emotional and psychological mood;
- the current situation;
- external factors;
- our culture, or the way we have been brought up.

To understand more about our perception, let us look at these a little closer. The first time we meet someone new we will subconsciously form an instant opinion. This impression is gained from the way he or she looks, talks, smells and reacts to us: so it is the reaction of our sensory organs. Equally, our mood will affect our opinions: whether we are in a good or a bad mood alters our responsiveness to other people.

The situation has some bearing: for example, in an interview our senses will be more alert and we will take in more, but at the same time we are likely to be feeling nervous and unsure.

External factors influence our opinion. Group pressure can be a key factor: we tend to think and react according to the company we are in, particularly as most people don't want to differ in opinion from their colleagues. Another psychological barrier that subconsciously affects our perception is stereotyping. We tend to put people into boxes and then find it difficult to differentiate between the box and the individual person. For example, think of a policeman: you will automatically think of his uniform and his lawful manner; you will not naturally think about or even see the person inside. This can cause a mindblock, blinding us to any individual potential, and this emphasizes the need for perception awareness.

The way we have been brought up plays a strong part in perception. We are taught how to react to certain situations from a very early age: children that have grown up with plenty of affection will naturally be more affectionate and tactile, and this will later affect their perception of other people.

Culture is very important, and if you work in an international environment it is essential to understand different cultures and to be adaptable. Some actions could be taken as being overly familiar or offensive, yet to some nationalities they are part of a business behaviour pattern. For example, an Englishman will usually just greet another colleague verbally; a Frenchman will certainly shake hands; a German will greet very formally; a Spaniard or Italian is likely to hug; some Americans are startled by touch.

It is very important to become aware of perceptions – both yours and those of people around you – and to learn how to manipulate these perceptions for your own benefit. This is particularly useful in the working environment.

Some professional organizations manage people's perceptions of them in various ways. Think of McDonald's fast food restaurants: they have a reputation for cleanliness because they always have staff who appear to be clearing tables. Another example is a London borough where a couple of employees can be seen every other morning sweeping the road that leads to the station during commuter time: this gives people living in the borough the impression that their roads are being regularly cleaned and they feel satisfied that they are getting something for their rates. For all they know, the cleaners only work that one half-hour a day and that is the only street that is cleaned – but it is the perception that counts.

As a simple analogy, think of two secretaries at different desks: one is a tidy person with no papers visible, the other is naturally untidy with a messy desk piled high with documents. To the uninitiated the immediate perception is that the first person has nothing to do, whereas the second person is incredibly busy. This probably isn't true at all, but the way the two individuals have come across is simply because of their different working habits and the perceptions they arouse.

You can learn to manage other people's perceptions of you effectively. There will be times when you may not be overworked, but still want to give the impression you are busy. After all, no one values an employee who sits reading magazines or filing nails, or who generally has nothing obvious to do. In these rare circumstances, you want to appear to be gainfully employed, and others' perception of you can be easily controlled.

You may be someone who works very well with a messy desk, but it gives the impression of being unprofessional. Try to put your papers into tidy piles – it doesn't even matter if the piles are not sensibly organized (as long as you can find what you need), but it will create the impression that, although you are busy, you are also organized.

If you work on a terminal, it is an idea to ensure that you always have a document on the screen (although do ensure it is not of a confidential nature). This will also create the illusion that you are busy, while a blank screen will indicate the opposite. If you are going into a meeting or even just going to chat to someone for a few minutes, carry a folder or notebook and pen. This makes you look more efficient and professional.

There are many more ways of which you will become aware that will help you to increase the professionalism of the image you portray.

Communicating with Other People

Communication is a two-way process used to exchange information and ideas, pass on knowledge and share thoughts and feelings. It is an important part of any role and can have a serious impact on a business's reputation.

We communicate with each other through three different channels:

- the words we say;
- the tone we use;
- the way we say the words (or our body language).

A useful adage to remember is 'of whom we speak, to whom we speak and how and when and where'.

Naturally, face-to-face conversation is much easier, with less room for misunderstanding. We read each other's behavioural signals as well as listening to what we say and the way we speak. Telephone communication is therefore much harder and requires more effort to transmit the same message. To emphasize this point, look at the following statistics on the relative importance of the channels in telephone and face-to-face conversations:

	Telephone	*Face-to-face*
Words	20%	10%
Tone	80%	25%
Body language	–	65%

It can be seen that tone absorbs body language during telephone communication.

It is also interesting to note that however hard we may concentrate, we only actually listen and take in around 10 per cent of what we hear. Think of communication with each other as an interpretation of a message through code.

Now you realize how important it is to say what you actually mean as clearly and concisely as possible.

We should also remember that we have two ears and one mouth – and they are meant to be used in that ratio. So we should listen twice as much as we speak.

Listening

Listening is a valuable (and frequently underestimated) business skill. This involves listening not only to the words, but the way they are said – and what is left unsaid. Being an effective listener is essential in communication and it is vital to keep the communication channels as open as possible.

You can help the other party by being an attentive person to communicate with. Try to remember to listen carefully, and ask questions to clarify any points you are uncertain of and ensure you receive the maximum amount of information available.

Always ask open questions to invite more detail, rather than closed questions which only anticipate a 'yes' or 'no'.

In 1961, Dean Rusk said, 'One of the best ways to persuade others is with your ears – by listening to them.' Try to be an attentive listener:

L   look interested
I   information seeking: ask questions
S   stick to the subject concerned
T   test your understanding
E   evaluate the message you're receiving
N neutralize your thoughts against conflicts

Verbal Communication

The words we use

It is far too easy to open our mouths and say exactly what we think – particularly when we're in a comfortable atmosphere. But in a working environment, it is essential to think carefully before you speak, to choose words according to:

- what message you want to convey;
- who your audience is and their depth of knowledge;
- how long you have.

It is too easy to discourage understanding with jargon, acronyms, colloquialisms and abbreviations. Wherever possible and appropriate, it is best to use simple language.

Here are a few tips to help you transmit your message as efficiently and as effectively as possible.

- Use as few words as possible to get your point across. Don't embroider your sentences with flowery words and complicated phrases – they don't impress!
- Pronounce technical or unusual words slowly and distinctly.
- Use very simple language and speak slowly if your listener's mother tongue is not English.
- Use your own words: you don't want to come across as insincere or false.

In 1978 Sam Rayburn said that 'no one has a finer command of language than the person who keeps his mouth shut'. This is certainly a valid observation – it is often more effective to keep quiet.

Tone of voice

Our tone of voice is also vital. This is particularly true with telephone conversations, where it accounts for 80 per cent of the effectiveness of the message transmission. There are three key elements which affect the tone.

1. The quality of your voice:
   - volume (loudness/quietness);
   - speed (fast gabbling/slow monotonous);
   - smoothness (breathless/sing-song);
   - confidence (knowledgeable/hesitant).
2. Your attitude reflected in your tone:
   - cheerfulness/unemotional/unhappy;
   - authoritative/negative;
   - helpful/laziness and 'can't be bothered'.
3. The way you use your voice:
   - interrupting or being interrupted;
   - repeating (used to confirm understanding or through lack of attentive listening);
   - hesitation indicates uncertainty in your comprehension or lack of response.

You can adapt the tone of your voice to suit the occasion and alter the quality of your voice as you feel appropriate by varying the volume, speed and emphasis.

Body Language

Body language has become a prevalent communication method in our society. It is all about being able to read other people's thoughts and feelings through their gestures and through what is left unsaid instead of what is said. Naturally, behaviour patterns have existed for thousands of years, but it is only in the latter part of this century that people have started studying body language in more detail. It is incredible that while we have long been aware of the various signals animals send to each other, we as human beings have been so slow to accept the importance of body language in our daily communications with each other.

The Victorian parlour game of 'charades' is a typical example of body language as a means of communication. Charlie Chaplin was an early pioneer with his exaggerated miming actions to convey his intentions in silent movies. The silent movies themselves showed the importance of mime and gesture: the stars had to convey real meaning through their actions without the use of words. However, the concept of body language was given very little attention. It was not until the late 1960s that its popularity began to grow, and Desmond Morris increased awareness dramatically with his book *The Naked Ape*.

A research study carried out at the University of Louisville showed that more communication between humans takes places by means of body language than by any other method, with verbal discourse counting for only 35 per cent of the content of a face-to-face conversation and non-verbal for the other 65 per cent. We have an innate and sub-conscious ability to communicate through gestures and signals. For example, when we are happy we smile and our eyes shine; conversely, when we are angry or sad our eyes are dull and we frown.

It is also human behaviour to mirror each other's posture and actions if we want to gain acceptance. This is usually totally subconscious but is interesting to observe.

Some gestures can mean different things to people of different countries or from different cultures. However, much body language, particularly in Western society, is universally understood. We shake our heads to mean 'no' or 'don't understand', and we nod to confirm understanding and acceptance.

Women tend to be more readily able than men to read others' behavioural signals. Part of this ability is learned by a mother's awareness of her baby's or child's gestures for attention: it is a woman's natural attribute to be more altruistic and therefore more perceptive. Men are less aware, and will frequently not notice body language. How often has a wife remarked on the tension or unspoken conversation that is taking place in a room, of which the husband is blissfully ignorant?

There has been much debate over whether body language is innate or learned. Certainly through studying the people around us, we can increase our awareness and learn to 'read' their behavioural signals and to adapt our own behaviour accordingly. For example, someone giving a presentation can judge the audience reaction from the way they are sitting, if they are fidgeting (or not) and their facial expressions, and the speaker can vary his presentation appropriately.

It is a fascinating subject to study in detail, but even for a layman it can provide a valuable tool in communication. Your own personal body language can consciously be adapted to suit your environment. Your awareness of others' behavioural signals can help you to 'listen' and facilitate your understanding.

This technique can be extended beyond gestures and signals to the working environment, and the use of furniture or equipment can be used to enhance someone's position and to exert influence. Knowledge of this can be particularly beneficial in meetings, and we will look at this in more detail a little later.

In some jobs it is essential to be well versed in non-verbal communication. During the Second World War interrogation officers were trained to read behavioural signals when interviewing prisoners. Today many officials are trained to understand body language. Examples include customs officers, policemen and social workers.

Understanding body language

To begin to understand body language, we have to understand a little about ourselves and how we react to other people. We all have our own personal comfort zones: that is, the amount of space we like to have around us to feel comfortable. If someone steps within this invisible boundary, he or she is invading our territory and we may feel threatened or exposed. This personal space changes according to the people we are with, our relationships with them and the way we are feeling at the time.

Generally, our comfort zones are divided into three different areas, with the dis-

Perception Awareness

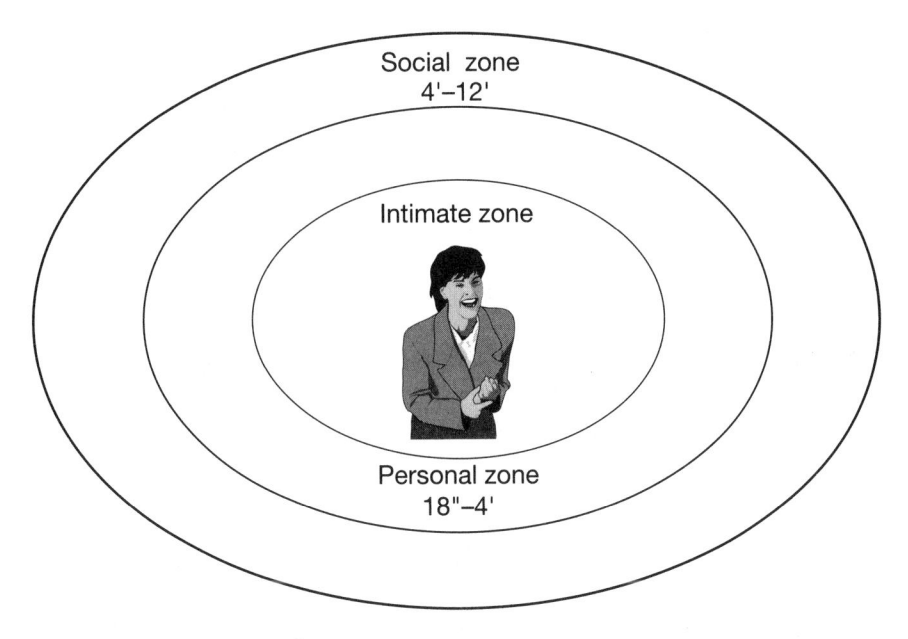

Figure 1 Our personal zones.

tance varying according to the relationship between ourselves and the other person (see Figure 1). Our immediate area is called our 'intimate zone' and surrounds us for between 6 and 18 inches; only lovers, parents, children and very close friends are permitted within it. Beyond this is our 'personal zone', up to 4 feet, with our friends, associates and colleagues allowed to venture within its boundaries; this is sometimes called the 'party zone', as socializing tends to be within this area. Finally, our 'social zone' extends to 12 feet, and this includes people we don't know well, don't like or don't feel comfortable with.

We like to own the territory around us and we don't like it invaded. An example of this territorial possession is frequently seen on busy commuter trains: wherever possible people sit on seats adjacent to empty seats, and they often discourage anyone sitting next to them by placing a bag or newspaper on the seat. Anyone who sits so close is invading our intimate zone, it causes us discomfort, we really don't like it and we will try to avoid it.

These zones tend to vary between countries, with many people feeling quite comfortable in each other's intimate zones. It is also interesting to note that people brought up in the city have narrower zones than those from the wide open spaces of the countryside.

In a similar way, we feel uncomfortable with tactile gestures. We are wary if someone we don't know very well puts his or her arm around us: this is again an invasion of our intimate zone. Only as we get to know colleagues and friends better do we learn to trust them and feel more comfortable about these familiar gestures.

This territorial ownership is not limited to our own person. We extend it to our family and to our possessions. We feel resentful if we return to find someone sitting in our chair at our desk – they are invading!

Now let us look a little closer at actual gestures and what they mean. You might be surprised to see how many you already recognize and understand.

Hands

Hands are the primary indicator of the way a person is feeling or reacting, as they are usually exposed and clearly visible. We already know that clenched fists express anger and open palms have always been associated with honesty and truth. An example of this is seen in the witness in court, whose right hand is held up, palm outwards, when he vows to tell the truth. It is not so much the open palms, but the way they are facing. Facing upwards and outwards indicates honesty and openness to other people. Facing downwards shows that the person is holding something back and has a negative attitude. Many believe that our palms expose our true characters and lives to those gifted in palm-reading, and in displaying our open palms we are showing that we're prepared to be honest. If hands are hidden, it means that we are lying or trying to hide something. If our hands are tightly clenched it can mean we are either angry or very upset; we clench our fists to try to shut other people out.

The man in Figure 2 is declaring his honesty. His 'take me as you find me' attitude is obvious in his open arms and outstretched hands. He has nothing to hide and wants to be accepted.

Figure 2 Open palms indicate honesty.

Hand actions tell us a lot about the way a person is feeling and thinking. Frequently a liar will cover his mouth with his hand and will not meet your eyes; alternatively he may run his fingers around his collar, indicating his feelings of unease. A worried person may bite his fingernails, or suck on his fingers or thumb: this is a reflex comfort-seeking reaction learned in childhood to which adults revert when they feel under pressure.

The way someone touches her face with her fingers is also very revealing. Interest is often expressed by laying one finger along the cheek or by stroking the chin. Hugging the chin or cheeks indicates boredom. Scratching one ear or the other shows that the person listening is not feeling comfortable: he believes he is hearing lies and is subconsciously trying to block out what he hears. If someone is feeling uncertain or doubtful, she scratches her neck. Rubbing hands together indicates joy or enthusiasm, the idea of really enjoying something which encourages us to rub our hands or to clap.

Look at the man in Figure 3 – he is obviously lying. He is running his finger round the inside of his collar, which indicates he is feeling uncomfortable. His eyes are looking sideways, away from the person he is with. His mouth is firmly shut.

The person in control will link his hands behind his head with his fingers interlaced: he feels comfortable, unthreatened and totally in control. If the hands are spanning the waist, the person is ready for action and impatient to get on with what has to be done. People who thrust their hands into their pockets are shy, while the ones

Figure 3 The liar.

whose thumbs are left outside are naturally more dominant and try to control situations.

We use our arms to show our reaction. If we stretch out our arms to other people, we are welcoming them and indicating our willingness to be honest with them. Folded arms can mean boredom, but are more frequently a defensive action to protect our body from something we don't like the look or sound of. If our arms are folded with fists clenched, we are feeling particularly hostile towards the other person. Frequently, we will hold other objects as a barrier in the same way that we fold our arms. For example, we may hug a book to our body or a woman may hold a handbag against herself.

Look at the girl in Figure 4 and her body positions. She is feeling very defensive – her legs and her arms are crossed. She is clutching a book to her, which may indicate that she is trying to put a barrier between herself and the other person. Her head and eyes are cast downwards and she doesn't appear to be interested in whatever is going on.

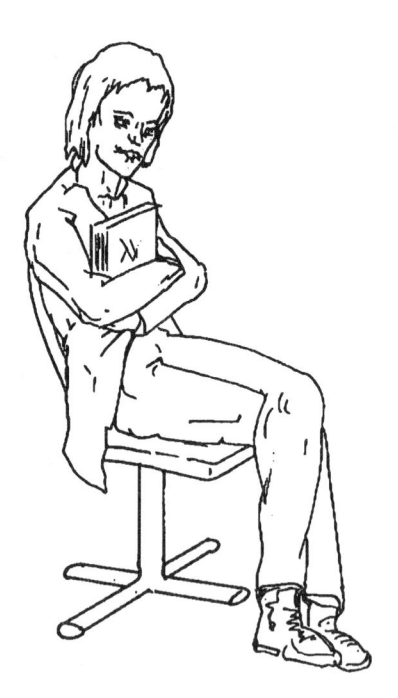

Figure 4 Defensive gestures.

Head positions

The head really has only three positions: upwards, downwards or to one side. So we tend to use our whole body to move with the head to communicate different feelings. A head tilted to one side and looking downwards shows a negative attitude, while if the head is tilted to one side but facing upwards we are being neutral and open-minded. We tend to show our disapproval or lack of interest by looking away, by moving our head in different directions or by glancing around the room – anywhere to avoid looking at the person speaking. If we are interested, thoughtful or considering a new idea we tend to tilt our head to one side. Perhaps the most obvious is leaning forwards: someone who is interested, enthusiastic and wants to be involved will lean his head and his whole body forward to try and get himself more into the conversation and to play an active role.

Figure 5 shows a man looking puzzled. His body language reflects that he is interested in what is going on, but doesn't fully understand. The finger laid against the side of his face indicates that he is thoughtful, obviously considering what is being said. He is leaning forward towards the other people and there are no defensive gestures of crossed arms or legs, so he is at ease in the situation. His facial expression demonstrates his puzzlement and desire to understand fully what is going on.

Figure 5 Looking thoughtful.

Legs

Leg gestures are similar to hand gestures in many respects. Crossed legs can indicate a negative or uncertain attitude, but it is important to remember that many women cross their legs all the time when sitting down for comfort (and frequently decency's sake). When combined with folded arms it is a sign that the person is displeased and

Introduction to Office Management for Secretaries

is adopting a defensive stance. Crossed ankles can indicate nervousness, particularly in an interview situation. Someone who sits with his hands gripping the side of the chair is usually trying to conceal his anger, while the person who has his hands on his knees is showing that the conversation is over as far as he is concerned and he is preparing to leave.

Many men cross one leg over the other with the ankle resting on the leg, and frequently grasping the ankle with one or both hands: this indicates a competitive or argumentative participant who wants to get his own way. This is further emphasized if it is combined with hands linked behind the head and leaning back in the chair: this person is in charge and subconsciously trying to intimidate.

In a similar way, someone who straddles his chair is often a dominant person who wants to take control of the group. He may feel slightly insecure and use the chair back as a way of protecting him from attack by the other people in the room.

People rarely stand with both feet on the ground and both legs straight. Often, they will cross their knees when standing and balance on one foot: this again can be a sign of nervousness, particularly with people in a group who do not know each other. The dominant person in control of the situation will stand with his weight on one hip and his hands on his waist.

Look at Figure 6 to see how this man is using his position to show he is trying to take charge of the group. He is seated back to front on his chair, using the chair back as a protective shield between himself and the other people in the room. He is lean-

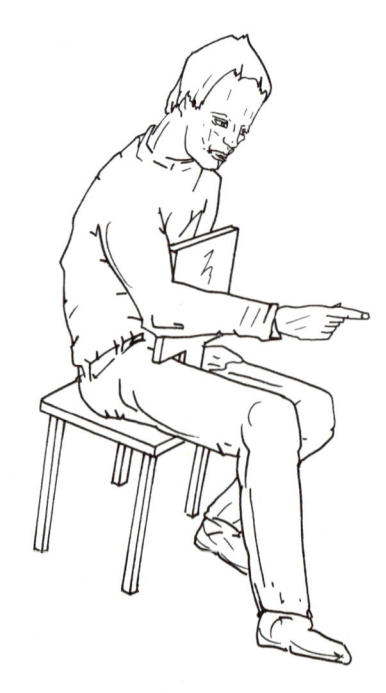

Figure 6 In control.

ing forward to show he is immersed in what is going on, his hand is raised and his finger pointed as if to say 'listen to me'.

Using furniture as props

Frequently, people feel more comfortable leaning against something. Leaning against a wall can indicate fear or nervousness: they are using the wall as a form of protection. Leaning on a desk is again a sign of territorial possession – it can sometimes be used to inspire confidence in certain situations, as the person thinks 'This is my desk, my domain and I am comfortable here.' In the same way, a driver will frequently lean against his car.

Office furniture can be used very effectively to promote our position. A typical example is the type of swivel chair found in most offices that have the facility to adjust the chair to a higher or lower position or alter the back. If we are seated higher than everyone else, we automatically feel in control. Frequently people will seek out these adjustable chairs and make sure they are at the optimum height. Similarly, someone who does not want to take an active part will be quite content to sit lower down and remain inconspicuous. This ability to be noticed is greatly assisted by the swivel chair: it gives the advantage of making the person mobile to move around the group and butt in between people.

A desk effectively puts a barrier between yourself and the person you are talking to. This can help people who are naturally nervous or shy as they feel safe within their own territory. Often we see managers comfortably seated in their posh swivel chairs, feet crossed and on the desk – this is a very clear example of the manager demonstrating ownership of his office and control of his territory.

On the other hand, the barrier can be particularly strong between a manager and an employee. It can be quite frightening for a candidate being interviewed by a manager seated on a higher chair behind a large desk. Many offices now use round tables to promote a sense of equality and to help with the manager–employee relationship, as research has shown that a round table provides a more relaxed environment and is far more conducive to team building and good relationships.

Figure 7 shows how a manager is using his position and the office furniture to show how important he is compared to the poor person he is interviewing. Note the large desk with his hands showing ownership of the desk; his chair is noticeably higher than the unadjustable chair that his visitor is using. His cigar is another sign of power – particularly in these days when smoking is seldom permitted in the office – and he is using it to demonstrate his authority. The visitor, on the other hand, is seated lower in a disadvantageous position. His hunched shoulders and his hands on his knees show his nervousness.

These are only guidelines to understanding more about body language and how we can use it to read the unspoken communication between people. It is a subject that invites a lot of interest and further study, but it is only through observing other people around you that you become aware of their behavioural signals.

Figure 7 The interviewer.

Eyes

Eyes are another key indicator of a person's thoughts and emotions. Often described as 'the windows of the soul', they reflect the way we are feeling. Eye contact is very important in face-to-face communication and tells us a lot about the other person. When we are interested or excited our pupils dilate, making our eyes appear larger. On the other hand, if we are feeling negative or unsure our pupils contract, discouraging open communication. Similarly, our eyes will be bright and attractive if we are feeling positive and dull if feeling unhappy. It is essential to establish eye contact with someone. Males and females tend to use their eye contact in different ways. Women are particularly skilful in sending messages with their eyes!

Also interesting are the various zones of eye contact, as these reflect the relationship between the two parties:

The forehead region:	Business discussion
Eyes and nose area:	Social conversation
Mouth and chin zone:	Intimate chat

Appearance and Attitude

We have already seen how we can manage our perception in a working environment and how we can become more aware. Similarly, how other people find us is influenced by:

- the way we look;
- the way we dress;
- the way we act and respond to other people.

When you meet someone new, it is your very first impression that affects the way you feel about him or her. Remember: 'First impressions count and you never get a second chance to make a first impression.' You should therefore try to convey a positive image through your appearance and your attitude.

Appearance

Consider the way you dress and the image you generally convey. A person dressed casually in jeans with untidy hair is unlikely to do well in a business office – no matter how good his qualifications. On the other hand, someone who is dressed neatly and is well groomed already has a definite advantage. Publius Syrus said in the first century BC that 'A fair exterior is a silent recommendation' – and that holds very true even twenty-one centuries later!

Although dress tends to be more casual now, with less emphasis placed upon it, it is still important to promote yourself through your appearance, particularly if you are seeking an executive secretarial position where appearance counts for a lot more. Looking after your appearance is very much a matter of common sense. Consider the following points to help you enhance your appearance and communicate a professional image.

- *Clothing:* make sure you feel comfortable in what you wear, but that you are not dressed too casually. It is all a matter of how professional you want to appear. For example, if you are a secretary dressed in floral Laura Ashley clothes, you will look neat and approachable, but it does not convey the impression of a professional person. On the other hand, a smart suit and crisp blouse will make anyone look competent. Although it is important to dress conservatively for the office, don't let it conceal your own sense of identity: if you like wearing bright clothes, do so – don't hide yourself in black just because you feel it makes you look more professional
- *Jewellery:* if you spend a lot of time exploring the inside of the photocopier or other machinery, think carefully about your jewellery – you don't want to hurt yourself or your jewellery
- *Shoes:* you walk around an office far more than you realize and it is essential that your footwear is comfortable and smart. If you have a long journey to the office,

you may consider keeping a second pair of shoes to change in to – particularly valuable when you get soaked on the way to work.
- *Hair:* must be clean and tidy. If you have long hair, it is an idea to tie it back or at least to ensure it doesn't get caught in printers, photocopiers or shredders when you lean over them.
- *Perfume:* should be subtle! There are few things more off-putting than very strong perfume when you are working with people.
- *Nails:* fingernails should be well manicured and, above all, clean. If you wear nail varnish, try to ensure it never looks chipped and uncared for. Clear nail varnish is very good for the typist as the chips don't show so easily and your nails still look good.
- *Make-up:* should also be subtle. Try to use make-up to enhance your appearance (particularly after a late night!) and not to change the way you look.

Whatever the image you want to convey, the skill is to look 'well cared for' and approachable. Your principal concern, however, should be to feel comfortable and confident in the way you dress.

Attitude

Of equal importance is your attitude, both to people and to your work. You should always try to emphasize the positive and eliminate the negative, to try to adopt a confident attitude and promote success.

We all know how off-putting it is when people consistently look on the bleak side: for example, the pessimist will claim 'it will probably rain today', whereas the optimist will say 'it may not rain today'. This is a very simplistic example, but demonstrates the difference between a negative and a positive attitude. You will also find that people naturally gravitate towards cheerful optimists; they do not need to feel depressed by pessimists.

Thinking positive thoughts will help you create a positive attitude. Remember the philosopher's words: 'I think, therefore I am.'

The way you interact with other people will communicate your attitude. Try to be friendly and open, smile and use your body language. Never forget that you should emphasize your tone and smile when you are talking on the telephone.

It is very easy to look downhearted when you are asked to do a difficult or time-consuming task, or if you are asked to work late. At these times it is particularly important to appear positive, no matter how angry you feel inside. You need to appear flexible, but the ability to say 'no' is also very important, so that you do not get taken for granted as a 'nice guy'.

Your attitude affects your appearance and your approach to people and to work. Try to make it a way of life to appear enthusiastic and confident. By being willing to help others, by acting as if everything you do is a pleasure, by talking to people, you will find that your attitude changes – and if you work in a group, this is most likely to rub off on other people too, making the office a happier place to work in.

It is very easy to let our personal problems invade our working life, but this is not professional and not tolerated in senior positions. No matter how low we are feeling, the place for personal problems is at home and they should be forgotten or put aside once you reach the office. This may not be easy, but try to think about the next person who rings you, or comes over to your desk with a query: she is an innocent victim who does not deserve to have the anger or unhappiness you are feeling directed at her. Often you will find that in 'putting a brave face on it', you will soon begin to feel better yourself. Likewise, you should try to understand and tolerate other people, who may not always feel as cheerful as they sound.

The power of positive thinking should never be underestimated. Homeopathy is a good example of this: although there are only tiny amounts of chemicals involved, homeopathic medicine will work for many people simply because they believe it will work. The successful people are those who believe they can make it happen.

You should never be afraid to admit you are wrong. Making mistakes is human, and admitting you have forgotten something is only natural – people will think more of you for it. Remember it does not matter how many times you fall over – it is how you pick yourself up that counts.

Remember Mary Kay Ash's words from 1985: 'If you think you can, you can. And if you think you can't, you're right.'

Your attitude is not just about being positive. You need to be flexible; in both the duties you carry out and the way you do them. Trying to adopt an open mind is not always easy, yet often we will find a more effective way of doing something if we are prepared to listen. Someone once told me that a willingness for routine tasks like making coffee is just as important as a willingness for the more glamorous jobs. This flexibility and willingness should be an important part of your attitude.

At the same time, you need to be assertive, to be able to say 'no' – and mean it. Assertiveness should not be confused with aggression. Aggressive people will deter other people and lose relationships as a result; assertive people simply appear confident and self-assured without impacting relationships.

In the same way, a secretary needs to be tactful. This is not always very easy, but you soon become adept at manipulating the truth to protect your manager when necessary. Loyalty is the most valuable and important quality in a secretary. Above all you need to be discreet and loyal to your boss and to your company. This will frequently require a lot of diplomacy! Try to stick as close to the truth as possible and, at the same time, sound as convincing as you are able. As Howard Newton said in 1988, 'Tact is the art of making a point without making an enemy.'

Finally, remember Peter Honey's words: 'Behaviour breeds behaviour.' If you can treat people the way you would like to be treated, you cannot go far wrong.

Self-management

To be effective and efficient in your job requires a certain amount of 'self-management'. This involves the way you manage yourself, your time and your working processes to ensure the job is done and you achieve job satisfaction. By learning new skills and improving the way you organize yourself, you will become more professional.

Here we look at the following self-management skills, which form the basis for a positive working style.

- Making the best use of your time.
- Organizing your working environment.
- Developing your own working strategy.

Making the Best Use of Your Time

Time management is a very fashionable concept among all companies, with courses available to increase your ability to manage your time effectively. Yet time management is really all about making the best possible use of the time available to you.

Franklin D. Roosevelt once said: 'Never before have we had so little time in which to do so much.' Surely, he must have been talking about secretaries when he uttered these words! Secretaries need to be good time managers – how else can they expect to control diaries and arrange meetings for other people? It is important to plan your time effectively to achieve everything that needs to be done.

We have all heard that 'work expands to fill the time available for its completion', and this further emphasizes the need for discipline. You never 'find' time for all the things you want to do, you have to 'make' time by planning your schedule effectively.

If you have a general problem with time – for example, getting to work or meetings on time – forward planning can help enormously. Always think in advance about what you will need and prepare accordingly. Know what time you need to leave and aim to be ready ten minutes beforehand. Just the simple trick of setting your watch five minutes fast may mean you will make an appointment you would otherwise have missed.

If you find that you do not have sufficient time to get everything done, but you find it is difficult to define exactly where your day has gone, try to keep a log of your daily work activities – each task and how long it takes you. You'll be surprised to find how much you fit into a day. You should also realize where you can save some time.

Prepare a list of 'common' activities (for example, dealing with mail, diary and meeting arrangements, typing correspondence, photocopying, sending faxes, administrative tasks, any meetings), or use the sample log in Figure 8 and note any additional tasks that occur or special projects you may be working on. Choose a typical working day and endeavour to keep track of how long you spend on each activity. Certainly you will notice the amount of time taken by answering the telephone and making calls. Use your log to look at how you could organize your day to help you make better use of your time.

DATE:			
Activity	**Time started**	**Time finished**	**Time taken**
Handling correspondence			
Diary			
Meeting arrangements			
Organizing travel			
Typing/word processing			
Photocopying			
Sending faxes			
Updating records/general admin.			
Filing			
Answering the telephone			
Making telephone calls			
Dealing with queries			
Taking dictation			
Meeting people			

Figure 8 Example of daily activity log.

The following hints may help you make the most of your time.

- Allocate set periods of time each day to:
    make telephone calls;
    deal with the mail;

Introduction to Office Management for Secretaries

  sit down with your manager;
  handle administrative duties (filing, etc.);
  control diaries.
- Evaluate the time needed for a specific project, set that amount of time aside and get on with it.
- Set yourself deadlines that are prior to any actual deadlines you need to meet. If you can work to your own deadline, it gives you a certain sense of achievement. If you do not meet this cut-off point there is no need to worry as you still have time available before the official deadline.
- Try to do the smaller tasks as they arrive on your desk. Often they only take a couple of minutes and it avoids building unnecessary piles which will then take longer to process.
- Put papers in your filing system as you work. It prevents a build-up of filing.
- Try to get the mundane tasks out of the way first, enabling you to clear your desk area and concentrate fully on any major projects.
- Keep an itemized 'To do' list with a date and time for each item to be completed (see Figure 9). Tick them off as you go: it will make you realize how much you can accomplish when you set your mind to it.
- Learn to delegate tasks that you really don't need to do and which could just as easily be done by someone else. You should try to delegate some of the more time-consuming tasks – not just the ones you don't enjoy doing.
- Plan your day, your week and your month according to deadlines that need to be met.
- Set aside an hour a day to make any telephone calls that need to be made: make sure you are fully prepared and try to get all the calls done at one time.
- Try to organize your boss to ensure he is aware of your time constraints as well as his own.

Date	Activity	Deadline	Done

Try to keep a daily list and tick off the activities as you complete them.

Figure 9 Example of a 'to do' list.

- Learn to handle the pressure from additional workloads by prioritizing according to urgency and necessity.
- Take time out for yourself; make sure you take regular breaks, no matter how short, to recharge your energy.
- Learn to handle interruptions gently, but firmly.
- Learn to say 'no' – and mean it.

Of course, interruptions will always occur – and always when you least need them. It is very hard to ignore a ringing telephone, or to discourage people from interrupting you for business reasons or a social gossip. There is very little you can do to prevent these interruptions, yet if you learn to manage your own time, you'll find that these small disruptions will have a lower impact. Above all, never use an interruption as an excuse!

Finally, remember John Meskiman's words from 1974: 'There's never time to do it right, but always time to do it over.'

Handling Workload Pressure

Workload is rarely a constant phenomenon in any job. There will always be peaks and troughs, and you will need to find out the working cycle in your own job and work out the best way to handle it.

For example, you may find that before certain meetings or events, your workload will increase significantly, perhaps owing to the additional preparation required or perhaps owing to the requirements that a number of visitors could put on your time and available resources. Learn to plan for these peaks by getting all the less important tasks done beforehand, or leave them until after the event, when you can concentrate on them more easily.

You may find that particular deadlines create a certain amount of pressure. For example, month end, quarter end or year end in many offices tend to be the pinnacle of pressure. Ensure that you are prepared to put aside all tasks that can be done at other times, leaving you free to deal with the pressure and the additional workload.

If you work for more than one manager, you need to develop a priority order for their output. This should be done by deference to seniority, but always bear in mind the actual task. For example, if it is customer-directed, it should take priority. However you choose to prioritize, you need to ensure that no one is unhappy with the service you are providing; explain your reasons for prioritizing and ensure the person understands the pressure you are working under.

Try to apply a 'pecking order' to your workload and categorize tasks according to importance. For example:

5 Immediate action calling for top priority.
4 Urgent: slot into workload within one hour.
3 Fairly important: complete within the day.

2 Unimportant: should be delegated or done during the week.
1 No importance: dismiss as irrelevant or wait until you're really bored.

Plan your working cycle according to the demands of the job and the pressures these will in turn create. This is a little like planning your budget over a certain amount of time: for example, ensuring that your salary will last until the next pay day.

Many people find they perform much better when working under pressure. Others find it is a very difficult and unacceptable part of the job. You can use the workload pressure to motivate yourself and increase your stamina, but be careful not to succumb to the pressure around you, as this can lead to job stress, illness and a deteriorating sense of achievement. It is therefore important to find a balance that suits you, your boss and the job. Remember, no one will gain if overwork and stress cause you to be bad tempered and slack in your job. Learn to moderate your working tempo and never be afraid to ask for help if you need it.

John Dos Passos said in 1959 that 'People don't choose their careers, they are engulfed by them.' This is very true; we all know people whose work totally envelops their lives to the point that they have no time or enthusiasm for anything or anyone else. No matter how important your job is, it is vital to keep a strict balance in your life.

Organizing Your Working Environment

It is important to organize your working environment so that you can quickly and easily find things you may need at a moment's notice. Planning your desk and working space effectively means being able to access anything and everything you may need with the minimum movement and therefore with minimum disruption.

You are likely to spend around eight hours a day at your desk, so make it a 'comfortable' place to be. Most desks today tend to be 'L-shaped', which gives you two working surfaces. Try to organize these so that one contains everything you may need to get at easily, and the other is free for a working area.

Also important is the position of your chair, the type of chair you use and the way you sit. Your chair needs to be comfortable; it needs to be on casters that will enable you to move around easily without any awkward movements; it should give support to your back and be of the correct height to enable you to type and work for long periods of time without discomfort. Many secretaries suffer from RSI – repetitive strain injury – particularly to the wrists, fingers and hands. This is usually owing to the typing position and the way you are sitting. Try to avoid any unnecessary stress on your joints by learning to sit correctly.

You will probably find you have some sort of terminal or PC on your desk. Try to position this in the corner of the 'L': it will take up less space and is easier for you to work at from an ergonomic point of view.

Self-management

Your telephone should be in a convenient position where you can get at it quickly and easily, as well as being in a comfortable position if you are expected to use the telephone as a dictating machine. In these instances, if you find yourself frequently balancing the receiver between your ear and your shoulder while your fingers type frantically, it could be a good idea to get a telephone rest to remove the stress to your neck and make it more comfortable for you when taking dictation.

It is best to think of all the items you need to access most often, sit at your desk and plan your space accordingly. You may also need to be accessible and facing a certain area: for example, you may find yourself seated near a door or an office, so you need to be in a position to see what is going on, if this is part of your job.

You will probably need one or two pedestals of drawers to fit under your desk to keep your things in. Your filing cupboards should not be too far away from your area either, so that you will not waste too much time away from your desk and your telephone, while searching through files.

Once your desk furniture and location are established, with the main items in place, you need to think about the items you need most often. For example:

- your in-tray – this should be on your desk;
- stationery items – paper, envelopes, complement slips;
- pens, pencils, highlighters and rulers;
- diary;
- message pads, Post-it pads and notebooks;
- scissors, letter-opener;
- glue, cellotape, Blutac, drawing pins;
- marker pens, flipchart pens;
- stapler, staples, paper clips and bulldog clips;
- Tippex and erasers;
- wastepaper bin.

Naturally, you will want to organize these items according to use. For example, you will want your message pad and pens close to the telephone. Stationery items, paper clips, scissors, etc. are best kept in a small tray in your top drawer – it is easier to keep them tidy.

You will also need to have easy access to:

- bring-forward system;
- diskettes;
- dictionary, thesaurus, telephone directories or other reference books;
- calculator;
- timetables (rail, air, etc.);
- atlas and road maps (A–Z if you work in London);
- address book or file;
- record box of index cards;
- forms (regularly used);

Introduction to Office Management for Secretaries

- certain files;
- telephone dial code booklet.

Use your drawers and conveniently placed shelves to arrange these items. Make the most of plastic folders and hanging folders to keep stationery, books and forms tidy and easy to find.

It is most important that your desk area is not cluttered and that you can easily lay your hands on what you may need. And always try to tidy up before you go home in the evening – there is nothing more off-putting in the morning than facing a messy pile of work. Edwin Bliss said in 1986 that 'A tidy desk encourages concentration; a dishevelled one is a psychological roadblock.' This is very true.

Secretaries are frequently asked for 'useful' things and you may need to keep a few extra items in your drawer. For example:

- a bottle of aspirin or paracetemol (check with your company policy before giving these to anyone);
- plasters;
- loose change (for parking meters and coffee machines);
- stamps;
- vending machine tokens;
- pocket sewing kit and safety pins;
- tissues.

Once you are happy with your desk, think about other things you need to be able to see at a glance. Make lists and pin these to partitions around your desk. For example, you may need:

- useful telephone numbers;
- useful fax numbers;
- workplan;
- yearly calendar;
- list of deadlines;
- organization charts;
- currency conversion tables (for frequent travellers).

Remember, it is no good putting lists up if you're not prepared to keep them up to date. Let's look in more detail at the above and how you can organize yourself with this valuable information:

- *Useful telephone numbers*: should contain numbers of people you frequently contact, both inside the company and outside – other secretaries, travel agency, railway stations, taxi firm, local restaurants, courier, accounts, payroll, security, maintenance, first aid, i.e. people you and your manager regularly communicate with. Keep separate lists of mobile telephone numbers and pager numbers. You will also need a departmental extension number list.
- *Useful fax numbers*: the same information as above.

	Monday ../../..	**Tuesday** ../../..	**Wednesday** ../../..	**Thursday** ../../..	**Friday** ../../..
A N Other					
J Bloggs					
F Smith					
C Green					
D Black					

Figure 10 Example of a workplan.

- *Workplan*: make up a workplan on a weekly basis in advance for the people you deal with so that you know where they will be, where they can be contacted and when they will be back in the office. Circulate the plan to anyone else who may need this information: for example, other secretaries, switchboard or reception. This will particularly help with telephone message taking.
- *Yearly calendar*: at the beginning of the year mark all important events, meetings, holidays and bank holidays (include US and European bank holidays if you work in an international department) on a wallchart or calendar. Use coloured stickers to add impact and easy recognition: for example, using blue for customer events, red for internal, green for training programmes, yellow for holidays, etc. Establish a system and then try to persuade other people in the office to adopt the same colour system, so that whichever office you happen to be in you will be able to 'read' the calendar.
- *List of deadlines*: keep a list of deadlines to be met and cut-off dates for departments like payroll, personnel and expenses. You will frequently need to refer to this and it is easiest if it is on your noticeboard.
- *Organization charts*: organization charts should contain the names, titles, locations and telephone numbers of everyone in the department or associated with the department. They should indicate reporting lines and dotted line responsibilities. It is useful to include names and telephone numbers of secretaries too. Remember, organization charts change very quickly and it is therefore imperative that they are kept as up to date as possible.
- *Currency conversion charts*: if your manager is a frequent traveller, you may find it useful to keep a list of common currency conversion charts. You can find these in newspapers or travel agents and photocopy to a reasonable reading size. You may also find it useful to keep a list of international time differences for any international telephone calls.

Developing Your Working Strategy

We have already looked at making the best use of your time. Now we need to look at developing your own working strategy. By assessing the needs of your job and your own role, you will see that certain procedures need to be followed and other processes need to be established. You may find that certain documentation will help you.

All organizations have particular ways of doing things and you may find that they suit you or that you can find a better, more efficient way of doing a job. Never be afraid to make changes. As Robert Burton commented, 'No rule is so general, which admits not some exception.' Use your own ideas and experience to develop working processes to suit yourself and your job.

Documenting your procedures can help both you and your fellow workers. It is a good idea to make up a 'secretarial bible', which could include, for example,

- working procedures;
- instructions on using any systems;
- list of files;
- organization charts, telephone numbers, etc.;
- company procedures;
- company or departmental procedures;
- checklists for daily, weekly or monthly duties;
- meeting procedures (attendees, venues, dates, etc.).

Not only would this provide you with a valuable reference tool, but it would assist anyone taking over your job during holiday or sickness absences, ensuring that the office will run smoothly while you are away and you do not return to a pile of work.

Checklists can be a very useful *aide-mémoire* to remind you of the tasks which need to be done on a regular basis. Make lists of daily, weekly and monthly duties which you need to carry out. For example:

Daily checklist
- mail is opened and handled;
- diary is updated and you know what is going on;
- bring forward is checked;
- signature book is signed and dealt with accordingly.

Weekly checklist
- filing is done;
- any outstanding correspondence/issues are followed up;
- a workplan is made up for the following week;
- any system reports are updated and run off if appropriate.

Monthly checklist
- confirm personnel details and update records;
- maintain telephone contact lists;

Self-management

- update customer files;
- update organization charts;
- maintain circulation and distribution lists;
- ensure any budget reports or forecasts are updated.

Day book

It is very easy to forget the little tasks that people ask you to do, particularly when you're busy or involved in something else at the time. Try to make a point of writing everything down as you go along. Keeping a 'Day book' can be very valuable. By dating the page, writing tasks down and marking them off when they are completed, you can use your Day book as a useful reminder for the little jobs you may forget. It can also be quite useful to look back after a week or so, if you are searching for information.

Organizing your papers

You will find that you need to keep one or more folders with current work in. Today's wide selection of stationery makes this much easier. You may find it is useful to keep three main folders, and these should be:

- action or work in progress;
- pending;
- filing.

You can colour code these to make them more identifiable. Plastic wallets are also invaluable in keeping papers together. For example, instead of clipping together all the papers for a particular meeting, use a plastic wallet to accumulate everything for the meeting and label it. Try to use different colour wallets for different categories, e.g. use red for meetings, blue for administration, green for work to be typed and so on.

Try not to keep too much in your current folder, but transfer into your filing or bring forward system. This will make it easier to handle and you will not be put off by a large pile of work.

Starters and leavers

You may work in a department which sees a rapid turnover in personnel. In this case it can be useful to compose checklists or packages for starters and leavers. This should include documentation on what needs to be done from an administrative point of view and from the employee's side.

For new starters to the company and/or department, you may wish to put together a package which contains, for example:

- company/department information;

- organization charts;
- information on company policies (smoking, pensions, car);
- guidelines on expense reimbursement;
- copies of any regular forms and instructions on completion;
- telephone contact lists;
- guidelines for using any systems;
- where to go for help;

This can help a new employee with the difficult task of starting a new job, settling into a new environment and finding out about the way the company operates. It may seem an onerous task initially, but once it has been compiled it can be fairly easily updated.

You will also need to know what you would have to do from an administrative side for a new starter joining the company. For example:

- find a desk and ensure it is equipped with stationery, storage space and a telephone;
- arrange for mobile telephone or other equipment as applicable;
- provide a mail drop or pigeon hole;
- advise reception and switchboard;
- inform security;
- set up any system ids that will be required;
- advise other employees of the new joiner.

You may also find it useful to draw up a list detailing actions that need to be taken when an employee is leaving the company. For example:

- retrieve desk keys and ensure files are left behind;
- ensure any company-owned equipment is returned (mobile phone, laptop, home terminal or manuals);
- inform security, switchboard and reception;
- block any system access.

The Professional Approach

Taking the professional approach means adding extra value to any task you undertake. It is really all about thorough staffwork: ensuring you find out all the background information you need before you begin to work through a problem. Providing a professional service means paying sufficient attention to detail; checking and double checking. It means doing a job and doing it well.

Anyone can organize a meeting, make travel arrangements, type a document, look after a diary or do the filing – but not everyone can do it well. You need to adopt a professional approach to the way you work and the tasks you undertake in order to provide a more efficient service and to promote your own professional image.

Remember the old saying, 'If a job is worth doing, it is worth doing well'? This applies to almost everything we do and we need to recognize this of even the smallest jobs. If we develop our own way of organizing and performing tasks, we can ensure that everything we do is done well.

With a little thought and preparation, you will easily be recognized for your professionalism and efficiency. The same lack of thought and failure to prepare will give you a reputation for your lack of attention.

Perhaps the best example of the importance of a professional approach to your work is the old nursery rhyme:

For the want of a nail, the shoe was lost; for the want of a shoe, the horse was lost; for the want of a horse, a rider was lost; for the want of a rider, an army was lost; for the want of an army, the battle was lost; for the want of a battle, the kingdom was lost. And all for the want of a horseshoe nail.

This certainly emphasizes how the smallest thing forgotten can cause everything else to go wrong. Think of this in terms of your job: if you forget to arrange the overhead projector for a meeting, the whole meeting will fail, as presentations cannot be given.

If you think about your role, you will find many ways in which to add value: to provide a little extra to show you are a professional. For example, consider travel arrangements you may be making for your manager's trip: when looking at train times, always give a choice of times either side of the most convenient train, write these down and give them to your manager with his ticket. This will help him if he is delayed for any reason and at the same time you are showing some thought and proving how efficient you are. This is just one example; you will find many more ways of adding extra value without it taking any more of your time.

In previous chapters, we have already looked at developing our own procedures for the way we work, organizing meetings, controlling diaries, arranging travel and carrying out general office duties. Yet for unusual tasks, we need to adopt a different approach and here we need to consider many things.

First, it is important that you:

- recognize the value of what you are doing;
- appreciate the need for background work;
- remain open-minded;
- display a positive attitude;
- be well organized in your approach;
- devote sufficient time to research;
- seek solutions (don't redefine or emphasize the problem);
- pay attention to time constraints;
- consider all alternatives and options;
- consult with other people;
- communicate effectively.

A professional approach is needed to ensure that you make more effective use of your time and that of those you are working with. It is valuable in broadening your own knowledge and gaining experience. Most importantly, it gives you the opportunity to use your own initiative and to prove how effective you are in the way you handle your role. This can make you stand out from the crowd and, in time, may lead to promotion or better prospects.

Frequently a task may be delegated to the secretary because a manager may be working on a more difficult job.

Let us consider these tasks as projects and look at various methods of completing a project successfully.

Projects

A project may be identified as:

- a routine task, such as defining a new method for looking after the departmental budget;
- a specific request from your manager, such as organizing a kick-off meeting for your department;
- an area for improvement in the working environment that you are aware of and undertake of your own initiative, such as establishing a reference library of documentation.

In all these circumstances it is essential to understand fully the terms of reference (TORs) before beginning your project. These can best be defined as:

- *objectives*: the purpose of the task and what you hope to achieve;
- *scope*: the boundaries of the project;
- *timeframe*: the length of time allowed for the completion of the project;
- *cost*: any cost incurred either during the project work or as a result of your final recommendation.

Once you have identified your TORs and you understand your requirements, you need to play your study and your approach, look at the various options and think through all the possible consequences. Finally, after your investigations, you will need to document your work and present it in a well structured, comprehensive format that shows all the details have been worked through thoroughly. You may choose to communicate your results in several ways according to the complexity and nature of the project. Your options could include a short verbal report, a written memo, a presentation or a written report. Whichever method you choose to convey your findings, remember to be positive, relevant and thorough.

By adopting a professional and organized approach to a project, you can ensure a successful conclusion. Often you may feel frustrated by your lack of knowledge or your inexperience: think of it as a challenge and an opportunity to prove yourself. Ultimately it will give you a great sense of achievement. Never be afraid to ask other people: this is the only way you can ever learn. At the end of your project, ask yourself if you would be happy with the completed work if you were in your manager's shoes – if you are satisfied, then you have done your best; if not, you should rework through your project.

It is best to adopt a systematic approach to a problem or project. Try to work through the following four phases:

- *Understanding the requirements*: you need to make sure you really understand what is needed when you are asked to do a task. Ask questions (how, where, when, why), query any points you are unsure of, seek clarification, confirm your understanding. Affirm the time scale of the project. Always make notes in writing – don't rely on remembering everything. Once you fully comprehend the requirements of a task, you can move on to the next phase.
- *Assessing the requirements*: now that you know what is required, you can look at ways of achieving this, bearing in mind time and budget constraints. List everything that needs to be looked at, find out all the facts and do your research thoroughly.
- *Evaluating the options*: now is the time to be open-minded and to try to think laterally. In considering all the alternatives, you may wish to ask other people's opinions. Try to list several solutions, each time looking at cost and time requirements. Think about the consequences for each option and weigh up what the reaction would be. Use your own judgement and never be afraid to quote your own opinions. Make your own decisions.

- *Communicating your results*: once you have weighed up all the alternatives, you should come to your own conclusion. Where this needs the approval of other people, you need to confirm in the most concise way possible to ensure cooperation. This could be through means of a written or verbal report. In either case, you need to define clearly the requirements, state the alternatives you looked at and recommend your own solution – backing this up with details of cost, time and your own personal reasons.

Let us look at this professional approach in a different way:

P is for Preparation;
L is for Listening to what is needed;
A is for Assessing the requirements;
N is for Need for attention to detail.

Planning is the fundamental ingredient for any successful meeting, event or project. In 370 BC, Plato confirmed that 'The beginning is the most important part of any work.'

Time spent on planning is time invested in success. You can never spend too much time planning, or overestimate the importance of this phase of any task. It should account for at least 90 per cent of the time you spend on any particular task; after all, the planning phase encompasses the research, considering all alternatives and making recommendations. All that is left is the decision-making – and with all the background work done, this should be an easy and quick task! Look at Figure 11 to see how easy it is to fail.

NO	YES
Make assumptions without considering alternatives	Seek clarification and evaluate all options
Ineffective planning and bad time management	Effective planning and good use made of time
No recommendations with inadequate backup	Good recommendations with effective backup
Poor communication of findings and decision	Good communication of decision and research
UNPROFESSIONAL ATTITUDE	**PROFESSIONAL APPROACH**
RECOGNITION!	

Figure 11 Problem understanding requirements.

As an example of adopting a different approach to a problem, consider the following story. When British Rail workers were carrying out weekly rail strikes a few years ago, a secretary working in Central London was asked by her manager to consider various options for ensuring that all employees could get to work on those particular days without too much disruption in either their professional or personal lives. The obvious solution was for employees to drive to another location where coaches would pick them up and bus them into London. The downside of this solution was the high cost brought about by high demand, lack of coach availability and the long delay that would be experienced through heavy traffic. The secretary thought again, and came up with two further solutions. The first was to use the river bus, which proved to be a cost-effective and efficient way of bringing commuters in from East London, but the river bus did not travel sufficiently far upstream to be of any real benefit. A final solution was to hire a helicopter to ferry employees in to work. As the adjacent office block possessed both a helipad and company helicopter which they were prepared to hire, this seemed to be the best solution.

This shows how important it is to be open-minded, to investigate all potential solutions and to decide according to feasibility and cost.

Now let us work through another example. Let us suppose that your manager believes it would be a good idea to send out a newsletter to your customers and gives you the task of looking at the idea.

First, you need to *understand the requirements*. So you would probably ask the following questions:

- frequency;
- number of copies required;
- who should receive it (what level of management, which customers);
- how long/short it should be;
- what sort of format;
- what material should go into it;
- how it would be put together, printed and distributed;
- who would have overall responsibility.

Second, you need to *assess the requirements*.

- You may look at feasibility of weekly, monthly or quarterly.
- Talk to sales people and consider their opinions on who should receive the newsletter – quantity and level of management.
- Look at length and format – newspaper style, one sheet flyer, could include diagrams and pictures.
- Consider what material should be included – new products, announcements on people, meeting and course information, future offerings. Think about who would write these articles.
- Bearing in mind the chosen format, what sort of paper it would be printed on (colour and quality options), whether it could be done in-house. Think about the

onerous task of distribution: is there a central function within your company that could cope with a large mailshot on a regular basis, could you handle it yourself, would a local printer be responsible for this? You need to consider the time and cost involved.
- Consider various people (yourself included) who would have overall responsibility for this. Think about the time scale involved, task of writing articles, printing and distributing.

Third, you need to *evaluate your options*.

- Decide on a reasonable frequency, e.g. monthly.
- Set up a recommended distribution list of names, titles, companies and addresses – here you need to liaise with the sales force.
- Decide on the length and format of the newsletter. You need to choose a suitable 'title' for it and select a size, e.g. two sides of A4 paper in newspaper format.
- Allocate article writers, ensure they are sufficiently knowledgeable and gain their agreement to write on a regular basis.
- Find out about printing and distribution costs, both in-house and external printers. Consider postage and stationery costs.
- Decide who should have overall responsibility for coordinating the newsletter, and gain their agreement.

Finally, you need to *make your decision and communicate your results*.

- Prepare a report or presentation with your suggested recommendations with back-up information.
- Involve anyone who may need to be involved with the decision-making.
- Seek approval or agreement for your project.

It may seem like a lot of work, but planning is the most important aspect of any task. Once the staffwork has been done and the ground rules are established, the project is likely to go ahead smoothly. Finally, remember: 'To fail to prepare is to prepare to fail.'

Use Figure 12 to help you with your project work. Now use the checklist for the four stages of your project to ensure you don't miss anything out.

Project checklist

Stage 1: understand the requirements

- Terms of reference – seek clarification and confirm your understanding.
- Ask questions – how, where, when, why.

Stage 2: assess the requirements

- List everything that needs to be done.

The Professional Approach

TERMS OF REFERENCE
Objectives:
Scope:
Timeframe:
Cost:

Figure 12 Project sheet.

- Find out all the facts.
- Talk to other people.
- Research and make notes.

Stage 3: evaluate the options

- Look for solutions – include cost and time requirements.
- Ask other people's opinions.
- Think about the consequences for each option.
- Make your own decision for recommendation.

Stage 4: communicate your results

- Decide on the method of communicating your results (written, verbal, presentation).
- Define the requirements of the project.
- State your findings and proposed alternatives.
- Recommend your own solution (include details of cost, time and reasons).
- Seek approval or agreement.

Customer Care

Now that we have looked at approaching our jobs with a professional attitude, we need to look at customer care and the way we look after our customers. Customer care is all about making the customer feel important and not just one of many. It aims to provide a service that exceeds the customer's expectations: to under-promise and

Introduction to Office Management for Secretaries

to over-deliver. This in turn will ensure he is a satisfied customer who will come back and who, more importantly, will tell other people about the excellent service he has received. In the same way, a disgruntled customer is sure to tell others. A good customer relationship is important for a number of reasons:

- to establish and maintain the reputation of your company and its product;
- to ensure follow-on purchases (or work);
- to protect your company from the competition.

So we must remember that:

- the customer is always the most important person;
- the customer may not always be right – but he is always the customer and should not be argued with;
- the customer is the reason you have a job – without his requirements there would be no company and there would be no secretarial job.

There are many ways in which a secretary can influence a customer's perception of the company she works for and of the product. It is frequently the secretary who is the first point of contact between a customer and the company, and therefore it is important to treat this first contact with care, consideration and politeness. Frequently this first contact is via the telephone and you should remember to:

- be friendly, courteous and helpful;
- call the customer by name where possible;
- be considerate and patient;
- ask questions and take notes;
- be willing to help;
- take your time;
- never promise something you cannot deliver.

We know how important our attitude and behaviour are and we have already looked at various techniques to improve other people's perception of us and the way we do business. Now let us look at how we can take this further and make our customers happy with the service we are providing. In dealing with customers, whether over the telephone or in person, you need to be:

- *Confident* – to give the customer the impression that you know what you are talking about and that you are able to help.
- *Committed* – to make him realize that he is important and that you are there to provide him with the best possible service.
- *Cooperative* – to be prepared to work with the customer to help him meet his demands.
- *Caring* – to show the customer you are genuinely interested and want to help.

These four Cs are the key to ensuring you have satisfied customers.

It is important that you understand all the factors that can influence a relationship between the customer and your company. Consider the following factors which have an impact on customer relationships.

- Personalities: everyone is different and this sometimes means that people clash.
- Professionalism: this comes across in all sorts of situations and can impress the customer either positively or negatively.
- Pressure: your company and your customer will have different demands; this could be on their time, on their budget or on their expectation.
- The company and the product.

No matter how good a product may be, it will not sell if the company or its employees convey a poor impression. In your dealings with the customer, you need to consider the following:

- loyalty to your company, the product and your colleagues;
- never infer that the customer is at fault or to blame;
- try to manage and condition the customer's expectations;
- educate your customers in the way your company does business – if they understand how your company functions they may be more considerate.

Now you can see how important customer care is and how much can stem from one impression. Taking all these things into consideration will help you to establish your own way of dealing with customers to ensure that customer care is high on your list of priorities. Finally, remember: 'it takes years to establish a good reputation ... and only minutes to destroy it.'

Quality Standards

We have looked at quality in our own roles and in the way we do our job; however, there is more to quality than the professional approach. Many companies and organizations now have certain quality standards that have to be achieved. These are quickly becoming standards that are laid down by external institutions and are common to all organizations. If a company meets these standards and complies with the regulations that are required, it can advertise that it possesses the external recommendation. This can be very important for many organizations: for example, a manufacturer making children's pushchairs needs to have an external standard to reassure potential customers that it is safe for young children.

The two main standards in the UK are:

- *BSI* – British Standards Institute, which is probably better known for its 'kite' sign which advertises that a company has met the quality standards it requires.
- *ISO* – International Standards Organization, which is known throughout the world.

Both organizations require very similar standards of quality to be met. The standards may include safety aspects. Some of the standards include documentation which is held in the office and for which you, as the secretary, may be responsible. Examples of these include organization charts, procedures documentation and customer complaint logs. All documentation must have a date on which it was created, a date on which it was updated, the name of the person who issued it and the name of the person who authorized it. If you are a secretary responsible for ensuring that quality standards are met in your role or in your department, you should request specific training from your company so that you are fully aware of the implications and requirements.

Working with People

Working with people is an inevitable part of nearly every job – and this is particularly true if you are a secretary. You will definitely be working for one or more manager in a secretarial capacity. You may be working as part of a departmental team made up of different people doing different jobs. You may form part of a secretarial team. You will certainly need to coordinate with members of different departments.

In any of these situations, we will always find that there are some people we get on with very well and others whom we believe we will never understand. Some people just operate on different wavelengths to ourselves and no matter how much effort we can put into a relationship, it will never seem to work. We need to remember that 'there is good in the worst of us, and bad in the best' – if we try to apply this age-old saying and look for the best in people, we will be rewarded with good working relationships.

Let us look a little closer at some of these working relationships and how we can make our lives a little easier by learning to get along with people better.

Your Manager

Your relationship with your manager is definitely the most important in the office; after all he is the one who pays your salary. Communication is the prime aspect of this relationship: you need to understand his role fully to enable him to carry out his job responsibilities, and he needs to understand the valuable part you play in ensuring the smooth running of his office.

Try to sit down regularly with your manager to get to know him as a person, not just a boss. Endeavour to find out his likes and dislikes and plan around these as far as possible. For example, he may be the sort of manager who likes early morning meetings, but likes to keep his time free after 5.00 p.m. He may enjoy long business lunches and social events, or find them a waste of time and money. By discovering these whims, you can make his agenda run more easily and keep him a happier person to work with.

Ask him questions about his partner or family. Try to find out about his children, their ages, birthdays, any special events, and make sure these are blocked in his diary – at least this way he won't be so likely to forget.

Find out his tastes. Does he prefer coffee or tea? Is he allergic to anything? Does he have particular dietary requirements? These will all help you in responding to invitations on his behalf.

It is helpful if you can organize your boss and find a way to work that will suit you both. Perhaps you need to sit down on a daily basis to discuss any current issues, to take dictation or to look at diary appointments. By organizing daily or regular sessions, you will eliminate any confusion or avoid potential problems.

Trust is vital between a manager and a secretary. You must know where your boss is at all times, so that you can cover for him if it becomes necessary. You must always be able to contact him in case there is a major problem. You need to define who you are talking to, before you give details of his whereabouts. You can hardly say he is at an important customer seminar if he is later spotted at the theatre with his wife. Nor should you tell his wife he is on holiday, when he is obviously not with her. Remember, diplomacy is the key word here. To be able to protect him and to safeguard his reputation, you, at least, must know the truth.

Many bosses look upon their secretary as their office wife: you are there to organize him, to make him coffee, to screen his visitors and to cover for him. Little touches like offering coffee to visitors and taking their coats should not be considered as demeaning – these are the extras that provide good customer service and make your visitors feel important. In turn, your boss should respect you as a person and not just as an extension of his office furniture. Be honest with him and you will find that your working relationship will benefit.

Your manager may have tasks that he can delegate to you, which make your job more interesting and take some of the work off his shoulders. Try to encourage him by displaying an interest, and ask intelligent questions. He will be only too happy to prove his knowledge, and you will learn more in the process.

Make your boss realize that he really couldn't manage without you . . . you are then in the best position possible and can reap the rewards.

Working in a Departmental or Project Team

If you work as part of a department of a number of people, you will inevitably be assigned the role of looking after all the administration side: fixing appointments, organizing people, sending memos – such is the life of a secretary. Remember, the secretary is the linchpin that holds a team together. Any team is dependent on good organization and communication. These are areas where you can excel. Think of the secretary's role in a team as a bridge: a number of bricks may go towards making a simple bridge, but without the keystone the bridge will collapse; your role is that of a keystone.

If you find yourself as part of a team working on a particular project, you will find that these same skills are very valuable and will be highly appreciated by other less efficient team members. Yet by showing some enthusiasm for some of the more interesting aspects, you can also take on a different role.

To get a team organized and running smoothly, it helps if you know the fundamentals of teamwork. First, let us look at the definition of a team. A team can be defined as a group of people working together with a common goal in mind. Each person has a specific role to play and a dependence on the other players. As a combined group, the team will succeed; individually they may fail.

A team is always composed of a number of different people. All bring different skills and different knowledge. To work effectively, you should put these individuals' skills to the best use. You will find that while one member may be very good at planning, another may excel at research, another may possess excellent 'salesman' skills and others are happy just to get on with the work they are told to do. As an example, look at the teamwork in a restaurant: a manager or head waiter will seat the guests, a waiter will take the order and serve the food, a chef will cook the meal and another person may clear and wash up. This is an example of teamwork and how different people with different skills make an effective team. If they were to change roles, the effect would not be the same and the customer would be dissatisfied.

At the outset of a project, when a team is formed, it is vital to assess what skills lie within the group and assign roles accordingly. Every team needs:

- a 'chairperson' who will be responsible for coordinating the group, assessing goals and making decisions;
- an 'organizer' or secretary who will be responsible for procedures and administration detail, ensuring that deadlines are met and that every member will be play his or her part;
- a 'salesperson' whose responsibility is to promote the team and to develop outside contacts;
- a 'planner' who will look after the research and planning side of the project.

Other team members are there to ensure the smooth running of a team, and that the staffwork is done. These people are no less important than key players, as they are frequently the ones who will do most of the actual work. When you are working in a team, it is important to ensure that everyone's voice can be heard. Try to bring in shyer members – their opinions are just as valid. Try to listen to people and be prepared to give in occasionally.

Teams will go through phases working together. At the outset they need to get to know each other and their particular roles. The next stage is to learn to work together, develop procedures and establish working habits. Finally the team will learn to work together towards achieving a common goal. This may require resourcefulness, flexibility, openness with each other, consideration and support of one another.

A successful team will:

- establish clear goals;
- compose a plan;
- define roles within the team;
- produce certain guidelines;

- communicate with each other constantly;
- consider all options and opinions;
- ensure active participation;
- make decisions together.

A team will fail if it does not consider all team members' opinions, if it does not look at all the options, if it digresses from the point and if the members argue with each other.

Now that you understand a little about the various roles of a team and the principles of working in a team, you will realize how important the role of secretary or organizer is. Your job is to coordinate, to deal with administration, to ensure time is managed effectively, with deadlines being met, and to set up effective communication channels. Remember, teamwork can be very satisfying and the more you put into it, the more you will get out of it.

Working in a Secretarial Team

It is quite likely you will find yourself working as part of a team of secretaries. Whether you work together to support one group of people, or whether you only sit together to provide cover and assistance, you need to be able to get along with the other secretaries.

Often you will find there are conflicts. These can be caused by different personalities, jealousies, ambition or loyalty to your own managers. It is natural to defend our own – whether it is our family, our dog or our boss – and to protect them. This is no different in an office: each secretary should be loyal to her manager, and you need to understand these conflicts to ensure a smooth working relationship.

Getting on with people is not always easy. Yet working in a secretarial team can bring all sorts of benefits: for example, in covering for each other, sharing information or helping with heavy workloads. Remember, you spend around eight hours a day working in your office and good relationships make for a much better working atmosphere.

Aim to find some common ground, talk about things you enjoy doing, sympathize where appropriate and always be prepared to listen. It is only through active listening that you will get to know people.

Never be afraid to ask for help or advice if you need it. You should never be worried about appearing ignorant, as everyone needs a helping hand now and again. This will show other secretaries that you respect their opinions and their knowledge.

It helps to be able to laugh at yourself too. If you make a mistake, don't be afraid to admit it and laugh about it. Then you can pick yourself up and try again. You will be respected far more than if you try to hide your faults and attempt to appear superhuman.

Working with Other Departments

Never think of people as being 'beneath' you. You may be your manager's right hand, but without people like postmen, receptionists, switchboard operators, maintenance men or security you would find your job a lot harder. These people need respect and affection too. It helps to be friendly: to share a joke, chat with them and show an interest. You never know when you may have an urgent package that needs to be sent at 5 o'clock on a Friday afternoon when the postroom is closing; or when your word processor needs repairing for you to get a large document out on time. You can guarantee they will remember if you have been rude or unfriendly in the past – and make you wait longer than necessary.

Establishing good working relationships with other departments is imperative. Not only will it ensure that you receive the best attention, it also conveys a very good impression of your department and your office. At the same time, you should try not to indulge in too much office gossip – secretaries can be a mine of good rumours and juicy gossip, but it won't do your reputation much good. It is important to strike a balance.

Communication

We have already looked at communication under 'Perception Awareness' and at how we can effectively communicate with other people both verbally and non-verbally. Today's technology offers us a vast array of communication methods, with telephones, voicemail systems, fax machines, electronic mail and video conferencing.

This chapter looks in more detail at these different media, how they function and their uses in the working environment today. It looks also at how we can enhance our skills to manage our communications more effectively and efficiently.

Telephone Communication

Telephone communication is a vital facet of today's business. Secretaries, in particular, spend a lot of time taking and making telephone calls, and it is essential to be able to use the telephone efficiently for maximum results.

The purpose of a telephone call is either to seek or to provide information, and questions provide the principal vehicle for establishing this requirement. Ask as many questions as you feel necessary and ensure you understand the responses. Telephone communication needs special attention, so focus particularly on your tone of voice and your words.

General guidelines when using the telephone

- Always speak into the receiver, but hold it a couple of inches away from your mouth so you don't unintentionally shout at your caller.
- Don't cover the receiver with your hand while you discuss the call with someone else – they can still hear you. Put the caller on hold (most telephones have this facility).
- Never eat, drink, smoke or type when talking on the phone – it can be heard and sounds as if you're not paying attention to the telephone call.
- Never conduct a conversation with someone else in the office at the same time. Your caller is paying for your time and deserves your undivided attention.
- When taking messages always take details of caller's name (ask him to spell if necessary), caller's company name, telephone number (including STD code), subject of call, date and time of call.
- It is a good idea to keep copies of your messages or use a carbonized message pad.

Answering the telephone

- Always make sure you have a pad and pen by the phone.
- Never let a telephone ring any longer than necessary – it generates frustration.
- Sound confident and *smile* when you answer the phone – the caller can hear a smile in your voice.
- Always announce yourself. The first few syllables are seldom heard, so offer a greeting first and then your name, e.g. 'Good morning. This is Anne Smith.'
- Find out who you are speaking to. Write the name down and use whenever possible throughout the conversation.
- Find out the reason for the call.
- Be as attentive and helpful as possible.
- Pay attention to detail.
- Ensure you ask sufficient questions to get all the information you need.
- Test your understanding by repeating the information, particularly if it is unusual or you're unsure.
- If you cannot help the caller, suggest someone who can. If this takes too long, take the number, name and subject and find someone to call him or her back.
- Always explain to your caller why you're putting him or her on hold. Never keep people holding too long; if necessary go back to them every 30 seconds or so to reassure them you have not forgotten them.
- At the end of a conversation, summarize your discussion, confirm any actions, thank the person and close the communication courteously.
- Always replace the receiver gently.

Making telephone calls

- Make sure you are properly prepared before lifting the receiver. You should always have paper and pen. You may need files or other material.
- Know what you are going to say, how you are going to say it and what you want to get out of the telephone call.
- When the phone is answered, introduce yourself, explain the reason for your call and find the right person to talk to.
- If you are providing information, state your points as clearly and concisely as possible.
- If you are seeking information, ask open questions, take notes and test your understanding of the responses.
- Always listen carefully.
- At the end of the conversation, summarize your conversation, confirm your understanding and restate anything you are unsure of.
- Agree your next actions.
- Thank your caller.
- Replace the receiver gently.

Handling complaints

Frequently callers ring to complain over the telephone: it is much easier for them than meeting someone face to face and they are therefore often more aggressive on the telephone. Remember – the customer may not always be right, but he is always the customer, and should therefore be treated with respect. Complaints are not always detrimental: they can be used as an excellent opportunity to improve your service and to demonstrate your and your company's efficiency.

Customer services employees, who handle a large number of complaints, are often trained to agree with the complainant at the outset of the communication. This can be a useful hint as it completely disarms the customer and deflects some of the personal anger.

Guidelines on handling a telephone complaint

- Be pleasant and courteous.
- Make a note of the customer's name and company. Use his name wherever possible.
- Listen to the complaint fully and don't interrupt your caller.
- Make a note of the complaint and keep a log of all complaints.
- Ask questions and summarize to ensure you are fully aware of all aspects of the complaint.
- Don't take the complaint personally – the customer is directing his anger at a situation, not at you. Put yourself in his position and try to show some understanding and sympathy.
- Never blame your company or processes. If the complaint is your fault, admit it and apologize. Denying responsibility will only cause the situation to deteriorate.
- Decide how you are going to action the complaint. Explain this to the customer and ensure that he agrees.
- Never make promises to the customer which you may not be able to fulfil. It's best to under-promise and over-deliver.
- If the complaint should be directed to others, ensure they are fully briefed before they call the customer back – this will prevent the customer repeating his complaint and feeling he is being pushed around an uncaring organization.
- Always handle the caller calmly, courteously but firmly.
- Show the customer you care and ensure he is happy with whatever action you are taking before you summarize and ring off.

Answerphones and Voicemail Systems

Many businesses now operate a telephone answerphone service or 'voicemail' when the recipient of a telephone call is not available. These tape-recorded messages can be very off-putting, particularly when you are not expecting this sort of response.

If you are the person making the call and reaching an answerphone, always remember to speak clearly, state your name, company, telephone number and brief reason for the call. Ensure your message is sharp and concise. Say 'thank you' or 'goodbye' at the end so that the recipient knows the message is complete.

If you are the person recording an outgoing message on your or your boss's answerphone, give as much information as possible. Always give the name, location where appropriate and, if possible, an alternative number that the customer can dial to reach someone who can help. There is nothing more frustrating than being a customer faced with an urgent problem and receiving an electronic voice that gives no valuable information. Update your message frequently and discipline yourself to listen to your recordings regularly.

An answerphone can be a useful tool in your office, but it needs to be treated correctly to ensure you receive the most benefit.

Facsimile Transmissions

Facsimile (or fax) transmissions have become an important part of office life, with the facility to transmit correspondence and documentation instantly to any other machine in the world. Papers are transmitted via telephone cables to destination numbers.

Before faxing documents you should always use a cover sheet which should give the following information:

- addressee's name, department, company and telephone number;
- destination fax number;
- your name, telephone number and fax number;
- number of pages including cover sheet;
- date and time of transmission;
- any information or comments needed;

Remember that a fax transmission is also a form of communication and the cover sheet reflects your and your company's working standards. It is advisable to prepare cover sheets with all the information for you and your manager and keep them handy – it saves rewriting the information each time.

Addressee:	....
Department/Company:	....
Fax Number:	....
Telephone Number:	....
From:	....
Department/Company:	....
Fax Number:	....
Telephone Number:	....
Date and Time:	....
Number of Pages:	....
Message:	

Figure 13 Example of a fax cover sheet.

Written Communication

Many companies have their own correspondence standards and it is necessary to adhere to these. All correspondence, whether letters, faxes, reports, contracts or invoices, is an ambassador for a company. Often it is the first impression a customer will receive and it should therefore be of the highest quality.

All documents have several components:

- customer reference;
- your reference;
- date;
- name of addressee and title;
- name and address of company;
- subject (possibly an additional reference or an account number).

References

References are an important part of a letter. They assist with identification, for both your company and your customer. If your company has its own standards, these should be followed. If not, you need to establish your own form of referencing. This should be sufficiently short to be uncomplicated, but comprehensible for you to follow and find correspondence again. It is useful to bear in mind that the maximum amount of characters that can be used to name a document on some word processing systems is eight and it is convenient to keep the reference and the storage number the same.

Here are a few examples of references which you may find would help you in identifying your documents.

- Author's initials/secretary's initials/number, e.g.: NS/AS/0001.
- Author's initials/date/memo number, e.g. NS/0608/01.
- Author's initials and number, e.g. NS0001.

It is often useful to keep a log of your reference numbers detailing:

- the reference;
- the date;
- the addressee;
- the name of the company.

Date	Reference	Author	Addressee	Company
10/6/97	NS/AS/01	Fred Smith	Joe Bloggs	Bloggs & Co

Figure 14 Example of a mail log.

Layouts

Layouts differ according to company procedure and use of pre-printed paper. Figures 15 to 17 give examples of layouts you may come across or wish to implement in your own correspondence. I would, however, point out that consistency in style is very important, and this should include the method for numbering continuation sheets.

49

Company letterhead

Customer reference:
Own reference:
(leave 2 clear lines)

Date:
(leave 2 clear lines)

Addressee's name
Title
Company name
Company address . . .
. . .
. . .

(leave 3 clear lines)

Dear Sir [or name]

Subject: . . .

Letter text

(leave 2 clear lines)
Yours sincerely/Yours faithfully

(leave 6 clear lines for signature)

Sender's name
Sender's title

(leave 3 clear lines)

Attached/Enclosed (if appropriate)

Figure 15 Example of letter layout (1).

Communication

Company letterhead

(leave 2 clear lines)

Date

(leave 2 clear lines)

Customer reference:
Your reference:

(leave 2 clear lines)

Customer name
Customer title
Company name
Company address
. . .

(leave 2 clear lines)

Subject: . . .

(leave 2 clear lines)

Dear ...

Body of text

(leave 2 clear lines)

Yours sincerely/Yours faithfully

(leave 6 clear lines for signature)

Sender's name
Sender's Title

(leave 3 clear lines)

Attached/Enclosed (as appropriate)

Figure 16 Example of letter layout (2).

Company name
Company address and information

(leave 3 clear lines)

Addressee name   Customer reference
Addressee title   *(leave 1 clear line)*
Company name   Your reference
Company address   *(leave 1 clear line)*
. . .   Date

(leave 3 clear lines)

Dear ...

Subject: . . .

Body of Letter

(leave 2 clear lines)

Yours faithfully/sincerely

(leave 6 clear lines for signature)

Sender's name
Sender's address

(leave 3 clear lines)

Attached/Enclosed (as appropriate)

Figure 17 Example of letter layout (3).

Today most companies have pre-printed stationery. Pre-printed letterhead paper takes a variety of forms, but all should include the following information:

- company name;
- company business (accountants, solicitors, etc.);
- full postal address;
- telephone number;
- fax number;
- telex number.

This will usually be at the top of the page, either centred or in the top right hand corner.

Often there will be additional information provided which is usually found at the bottom of the page and in a smaller print. This may include:

- registered company name and number;
- name of managing director or other;
- registered company address (frequently this will be different from the address at the top).

You will find that most letters are now placed in window envelopes. You should therefore ensure that the address will be completely in the window.

If you use a word processor, it is a good idea to set up standard letter formats to save yourself time and ensure consistency.

If a letter is continued on to two or more pages, they must be numbered. Continuation can be shown on the first page by using one of the following, which should be located in the bottom right hand corner of your page, giving at least two clear lines after the text:

- continued
- .../...
- cont'd

On second and subsequent pages, you should number consistently:

- – 2 – (centred);
- Page 2 (left or right margin or centred);
- company name (left margin), page number in right margin;
- company name with page number below (left margin).

Three clear lines should always be left before continuing with the text of the letter.

You should never leave widowed or orphaned lines (single lines at the beginning or end of a page). Neither should the second page just contain the closing greeting and author's name. Always carry forward the last couple of lines from the previous page and adjust spacing accordingly so that the finished letter looks well composed and balanced.

The address should be typed on envelopes or sticky labels (where larger or brown envelopes are used). When typed on envelopes the address should be blocked in the centre of the envelope. The name, title, company name and address should each have their own line. The town name should be in block capitals and the postcode should always sit alone on the bottom line of the address.

These guidelines help the Royal Mail's electronic sorting machinery to action mail more efficiently and quickly. If a letter is being sent by special post or air mail, this should also be indicated on the envelope on the top left-hand corner or centre.

If you are using sticky labels, ensure that all the address fits on the label – that the first or last line is not falling off.

Composing your own correspondence

If you are composing your own correspondence, you should always remember:

- The letter should consist of three main parts: an opening paragraph; the body of the letter (one or more paragraphs); a closing paragraph.
- Any letter beginning 'Dear Sir' or 'Dear Madam' should be closed with 'Yours faithfully' (and faithfully should always have a small initial letter).
- Today's feminism movement has created the title of 'Ms', intended for use by independent women. Although it can give rise to ambiguity, a general guideline is to use this form of address in correspondence when you are unsure of a woman's title.
- Any letter addressed to a person (e.g. 'Dear Mr Smith') should be closed with 'Yours sincerely' (and again sincerely should have a small initial letter).
- If you are inviting someone to ring you for any reason, ensure that your telephone number and extension number are included (if they are not already on the letterhead).
- Keep language simple and don't use words simply to impress.
- Keep to the point and avoid long unnecessary sentences.
- Don't begin too many paragraphs with 'I' or 'We'.
- Wherever possible, keep to one page – it is far more effective.

Finally, remember Jack Malby's words: 'Long words and complex sentences are intended to add importance to something unimportant.'

Office Practice

Mundane tasks such as handling mail, filing, preparing documents for signature and maintaining records form a large part of any secretary's workload. It is often one of the most boring parts of the job, but done properly it can greatly assist your efficiency.

These are the basics of any secretarial role and it is essential to develop your own method of doing things. Once your routine is in place, office practice becomes second nature, leaving you more free time to concentrate on the more important – and interesting – aspects of your role.

Handling Mail

Most secretaries will be expected to handle their manager's correspondence. This could be either paper or electronic mail, depending on the systems used within your company.

Handling the mail does not simply mean opening envelopes and putting the contents on someone else's desk. It should include all facets of correspondence and a professional secretary will be able to deal with around 80 per cent of the mail without referring to the manager.

Some companies have guidelines on what levels of mail should be opened by a secretary, depending on the level of the job and the nature of the business. For example, personnel departments need to be more circumspect on the number of people viewing correspondence. Here are some mail classifications which you will come across.

- Internal (company) mail: opened by secretary.
- External (customer) mail: opened by secretary.
- Confidential: opened by secretary.
- Personal: opened by manager.
- Private: opened by manager.

It is best to establish guidelines with your boss on how involved he wants you to be.

Mail should be opened and date-stamped promptly – as soon after the post arrives as possible. It is a good idea to divide into three categories. For example:

- for action – mail needing attention;
- for information – mail already dealt with or needing no action;
- for reading – items of general information, reports, trade journals, etc.

Customer correspondence should be given priority attention. If your manager is not available, someone else should be deputized to handle it in his absence. If this isn't possible, then send a holding reply explaining that a fuller response will be sent as soon as possible.

If a letter refers to previous correspondence, you should attach a copy, indicating on the original that you have included any back-up information.

If a letter needs to be redirected to someone else in the office, do so, but take a copy and note who you have sent it to: you may need to follow it up at a later stage.

If the letter is an invitation, check the diary and assess the importance of the event compared to other meetings already scheduled. Indicate on the invitation whether it is feasible and find out your manager's response before accepting or declining the invitation.

Most circulars and chain letters can be filed straight in the bin. It is advisable to glance briefly through circulars – you never know whether there may be something of interest or relevance.

Your manager may be very busy, with insufficient time to read the specialized newspapers, trade journals and reports that may contain relevant information. You may want to look through these briefly, and take a note of any articles of particular interest or value – for example, stories about your company, competitors, similar products, market surveys – and suggest that your manager reads only these.

Highlighters and Post-it pads are invaluable tools when it comes to dealing with correspondence. Use your fluorescent highlighter to mark important items. Use Post-it pads to make notes on what you have already done with the document.

Many secretaries find it useful to keep a log of incoming mail, which should include details of:

- date item was received;
- date (and often reference) of letter;
- sender's name and company name;
- subject of letter;
- action taken and further action required.

Bring Forward File

Bring forward files can be a very useful tool in making your life easier and proving how efficient you are – once you have disciplined yourself to use them!

It is no good diligently filing papers in your bring forward file and never remembering to look in it. You need to get in the habit of looking in your bring forward every day – first thing in the morning is probably the easiest to remember. If necessary, make a note on your calendar or diary.

A bring forward file is normally a concertina folder with a pocket for each date of the month, where you should file the relevant papers. It is a good idea to file documents in the pocket for the day before you actually need them – it's less risky if you're not that good at looking in your bring forward.

Bring forward notes can be used for many things. Here are a few useful ideas:

- to remind yourself of regular items which need to be dealt with (for example, a weekly workplan brought forward for every Monday morning, or a monthly report which needs to be completed);
- to file information relevant to a particular event or meeting;
- to remind you of deadlines or cut-off dates;
- to store temporarily information you are holding while waiting for additional documentation to arrive;
- as a chaser file for items needing follow-up or further action.

Record Maintenance

Records need to be maintained for both personnel and customer information. It is easiest to keep this information on record cards, filed alphabetically in an index box. This method is quickest and easiest to update and therefore more efficient than an address book. Many electronic office systems provide a facility for keeping these on-line, but it is also advisable to keep a printed-out version for times of system failure.

Employee and customer records need to be regularly maintained and kept in a secure place. It is imperative that the information is as accurate as possible.

Employee records

Employees' personal information should include the following details:

- full name;
- home address;
- home telephone number;
- personnel number.

In addition, you may find it useful to know:

- partner's name;
- children (if any);
- date of birth.

If the employee is your manager, then the more information you keep the easier your life will be. Additional details you may want to know are:

- Any credit card details (particularly if you need to book travel arrangements for him, as you will need details of his card, number and expiry date).
- Car details: make, model and registration number.
- Any details of memberships, e.g. frequent flyer programmes, institute member-

ships. You may want to make a note of the contact telephone number as well as the membership number.
- Any special dietary requirements.
- Any regular medication.
- Children's and partner's birthdays.
- Any useful telephone numbers, e.g. garage for car services, partner's work number.

The first four are particularly important if you book travel or respond to social invitations on his behalf.

Customer records

These should include:

- company's full name (and abbreviations if used);
- addresses of any branches you deal with;
- switchboard telephone numbers and any direct dial lines;
- fax number;
- telex number (if applicable);
- names and titles of people you deal with regularly;
- secretaries' names.

It may sometimes seem a chore to keep these details up to date, but in the long run they will increase your efficiency – you never know when your manager may need this information in a hurry.

Signature Book

Most items for a manager's signature will either be produced by the secretary or given to the secretary for processing. Before submitting anything for signature, you should check it thoroughly to ensure the following:

- the documentation is accurate (all fields completed on a form);
- prior signatures have been obtained, if appropriate;
- any attachment information is provided;
- any back-up information is provided;
- your manager is the correct signatory;
- any expenses are accurate and receipts are attached.

It is a good idea to highlight the signature field, print your manager's name and date the document if necessary. Items for signature need to be kept clean and flat. A signature book with blotting paper interleaves can be very useful. Checked documents should be placed inside and the book given to the manager once or twice a day (as appropriate). This will ensure that documents are not mislaid. It will also help your manager, who can concentrate more easily on what he is signing when the papers are presented in an orderly fashion.

Once documents are signed, always keep copies of anything you send out, particularly where these are items not created on a word processor.

Filing

Filing must be every secretary's nightmare. No one enjoys filing, yet it is an essential part of office life. Done properly it greatly enhances your effectiveness; poorly maintained it can cost customers.

Filing should enable any department member to find documents quickly and easily. It is no good operating a highly sophisticated system if you are the only person who can find anything. Always educate your manager and other appropriate personnel on your filing system.

Many companies have filing guidelines. Where this is appropriate you should comply with these guidelines. If there is no system in process, then it is best to develop your own to suit your own requirements. Establishing a filing system may seem a time-consuming duty, but it is much more beneficial to put a system in place rather than letting it simply evolve over time.

Today the electronic office means many documents are kept in softcopy format, restricting the volume of filing and the amount of time needed for filing. Yet always remember to keep back-up copies of your files.

Filing systems

Files can come in various formats, but the most popular is the vertical hanging folder with plastic tabs giving the name of the file.

These should be indexed according to your business. It is a good idea to establish main categories. For example:

- customer files;
- administration;
- employee files;
- correspondence files;
- finance;
- meetings and events.

These can then be sub-divided into as many files as necessary and filed alphabetically. For example, you may further divide your 'Finance' file:

- budgets;
- forecasts;

- profit and loss;
- revenue reports.

If you do keep softcopy and hardcopy files, try to keep the categories the same. You may find it useful to number the categories and sub-categories. For example:

1   Finance
   1.1   Budgets
   1.2   Forecasts . . .

Remember, filing is intended for easy retrieval: don't make your life too difficult.

Diaries and Travel

Looking after diaries and organizing events can be the most interesting aspect of a secretary's job. It can bring a lot of satisfaction when a well arranged meeting goes according to plan or reflect badly on you when things go wrong, as it is inevitably the secretary's responsibility. It is an area which deserves the greatest attention to detail and concentration, as even the most minor mistake can cause a major problem.

It pays to develop your own guidelines to managing diaries and to follow these scrupulously. In this way you can ensure you are planning for success.

Many managers still like to maintain a desk copy, which is the secretary's responsibility, and their own personal pocket diary. Today many diaries are kept on an electronic office system. This is of enormous value to a busy secretary. It is much easier to delete, move or copy regular meetings throughout the diary. However, there is a greater confidentiality risk and you should consider this aspect if you are looking after a senior manager or a personnel manager, who should not have a public diary. With softcopy diaries you may like to keep a printed version to hand so that you can quickly look at the diary when necessary, but do be careful not to double book any appointments.

Diary Control

A secretary will normally look after the manager's diary and it is advisable to decide with your manager how he wants you to control it. Find out how he feels about early morning and evening meetings; whether he likes breakfast or lunch appointments; if he enjoys social engagements or would rather get out of them, if at all possible. Discovering his wants and needs at the beginning can help a lot in planning his agenda.

A professional secretary will screen all potential visitors and filter as necessary. Remember, time is a very valuable commodity, particularly with the more senior managers and directors, and especially if they are key customer-facing people.

You should set yourself certain guidelines and establish a general 'pecking order' of priority. For example:

- existing customers first;
- potential prospects;
- higher level management;

- reporting employees;
- internal meetings.

Naturally you need to be flexible and weigh up each individual situation.

Remember to incorporate into the diary any social engagements your manager may be expected to attend, as well as any personal events: for example, school concerts, wedding anniversary. This shows consideration for him as a person and not just a manager. In some cases you may find you are expected to liaise with his partner.

Always leave sufficient time between meetings to allow for over-running. This will also give your manager time to clear his mind of one subject before focusing on the next appointment.

Henry Kissinger remarked in 1973: 'Next week there can't be any crisis, my schedule is already full.' This shows the value of allowing time for the unexpected crisis to occur. Effective planning in the first instance can save yourself a lot of time and effort in rescheduling meetings at a later date.

Never plan a day with back-to-back appointments if it is avoidable: your manager needs time to gather his thoughts. And it only takes one meeting to over-run to find the whole day's meetings go awry. You should also remember to allow enough time for getting from one room to another, or from one location to another. If there are a number of meetings that need to be scheduled in another location, make the most of your manager's time by booking as many as possible on the same day.

It is a good idea to set aside half an hour a day for mail, dictation, signatures and all the other office duties which can so easily be forgotten when meetings start filling up the diary.

Make your life easier and use the diary as a notebook too. Put as much information about a meeting in the diary as possible. For example:

- start time of meeting;
- planned end time;
- location (whose office, which building, which town, etc.);
- names of all attendees (including titles and company names where appropriate);
- subject of meeting;
- contact name and number of person setting up the meeting (in case you need to cancel or rearrange the appointment);
- any travel arrangements made;
- any prior briefing arrangements.

Try to look through the diary a couple of days in advance and confirm any meetings that may have been provisional. Consider if any briefings are necessary: for example, a salesman may need to brief the manager prior to a customer meeting. Schedule these briefings in advance or ask for short, but concise, written reports where it is more appropriate. This should ensure that your manager is well prepared and will not be wasting either his time or his customer's time.

At the beginning of a year, schedule all your regular meetings, ensuring they do not clash with any critical deadlines: for example, month end in a sales office. You may also want to note any key dates in the diary: for example, deadlines or your holiday dates.

Finally, remember Benjamin Franklin's words in 1748: 'time is money' and 'lost time can never be found again'.

Travel Arrangements

Travel arrangements need a lot of attention. When scheduling meetings in another location, town or country, it is important to remember:

- travelling time – and add time to allow for problems or any hold-ups;
- hour difference – if the meeting is taking place in another country;
- train/plane/shipping schedules – they may not always fit in with your arrangements.

If your manager needs to travel, then find out the most efficient method, in both expense and personal time. For example, it may be far quicker to go by train, which would also give him time to do any preparatory work during the journey; on the other hand, it may not be feasible from the point of view of getting to and from stations at either end.

When he is travelling by car, find out:

- the quickest and best roads;
- whether there are likely to be any roadworks or other hold-ups;
- whether there is adequate parking at the destination;
- whether it is the best use of his time.

When he is travelling by train, you need to know:

- nearest station to destination;
- journey time and schedules (both outward and return);
- travel arrangements for the 'other end' of the journey;
- ticket options;
- possibility of purchasing ticket in advance.

When he is travelling by air, you should ask:

- which airlines fly to the destination;
- which offer the best package;
- flight times and schedules;
- flexible ticket options;
- distance to and from airports;
- travel method to and from airports;
- any time difference;

- whether food is served in-flight (this may seem trivial, but if your manager is flying to Europe for an early morning meeting, he will most certainly want breakfast on the flight, and not all airlines provide this service).

Travelling by sea on business is unusual, but may occur from time to time. In these cases, you will need to know:

- length of crossing;
- frequency and timings of ferries;
- ticket options;
- destination and departure port preference.

If hotel or other accommodation arrangements need to be made, check the following:

- most convenient accommodation to destination;
- facilities provided;
- room rate and what it includes, including any special business or corporate rates;
- how to get there;
- car parking arrangements, if appropriate.

You may also need to arrange car hire at the destination. When booking the car you will need to know:

- your manager's driving licence number;
- type and class of car required – don't forget to stress if a particular type is required, such as manual or automatic;
- you will be asked for flight details if the car is being collected from an airport;
- duration the car is required for;
- time and place of return.

Don't forget that when your manager is travelling abroad, you should always check on the insurance aspect. This is usually provided by the company when an employee is travelling on business, but it is best to verify in advance.

You may also need to find out about any necessary visas or other travel documentation required before travelling to certain countries. Always confirm that your manager's passport is valid and will be for the duration of the trip. And, of course, certain countries require an approval letter from your company that the employee is travelling on company business.

Your manager may need medical injections before travelling to particular parts of the world and these need to be planned well in advance of the departure date.

Having assessed the best travel alternatives, think about all aspects of the journey and plan accordingly. Draw up a travel itinerary detailing all the arrangements made and alternatives where appropriate. Include items such as:

- place of departure (specify which airport, station, etc.);
- date of departure;
- time of departure;

- flight number or train code, if appropriate;
- time of arrival at destination;
- travel arrangements from place of arrival to meeting destination;
- any accommodation arrangements, which should include name of hotel, address and telephone number;
- any hire car arrangements made, include booking number and telephone contact number;
- return travel arrangements;
- contact number of travel agent or other who can help in case of problem or emergency;
- maps if appropriate.

If the travel is abroad, you will also need to find out about currency and probably obtain the necessary amount in advance. It is always best to check on credit card arrangements too.

Finally, put any documentation pertaining to the arrangements – ticket invoice, hotel confirmation, travel agent schedules, maps, timetables and tickets – in a clearly marked folder, together with your manager's itinerary and a copy of his diary meetings.

Meetings and Events

Organizing meetings and events can be a large part of your job. As with most tasks, the planning is the most important part and deserves the most attention.

Let us look first at what we actually mean when we talk of a 'meeting'. Fred Allen, in 1940, stated that 'A conference is a gathering of important people who, singly, can do nothing but together can decide that nothing can be done' – a humorous and apt description. More realistically, a meeting can refer to two people getting together or an assembly of hundreds of people, but the principle of any meeting is to bring people together with the aim of exchanging or presenting information, making decisions and signing contracts.

A meeting may be an informal chat over coffee, a business lunch between two or more colleagues, a formal meeting around a board table or a large gathering. If the need for a meeting has been established and there isn't a better alternative (e.g. sending a memo), however small or large the meeting is, certain arrangements need to be made. The more efficient the arrangements, the more effective the meeting.

Today, many media are available for meetings – for example, teleconferencing and videoconferencing – and you should consider these alternatives when scheduling a meeting.

Teleconferencing

Teleconferencing is the name given to a meeting that is held via the telephone. Today's telephones are extremely sophisticated and can offer a conference facility to link up two or more people so that they can hold a meeting and talk to one another at the same time.

Many telephones have a 'hands free' or 'speaker' facility. This means that all the participants in a room can hear what is being said and can speak into the microphone of the telephone instead of via a handset.

This is frequently used for short informal meetings and means that unnecessary travel and the associated costs can be avoided.

Videoconferencing

Videoconferencing is one of the most important and innovative advancements of computer technology in the office. Although it has been available since the early

1980s, it is only recently that videoconferencing is beginning to make a major impact in the office, because the cost of the equipment is falling while the quality has dramatically improved. It is without doubt the future direction for many business meetings and corporate communications.

Utilizing the same concept as teleconferencing, videoconferencing takes the process further, enabling participants to see each other and exchange data in addition to talking to one another. This means that the advantages of body language are incorporated and this effects a more efficient and honest communication.

Effective communication is essential in all businesses, and through the medium of videoconferencing, meetings can take place utilizing the techniques of multimedia. This means that meetings can be held without participants ever leaving their offices; this in turn leads to decreased costs, more effective use of time and greater productivity. Additionally, it means the potential involvement of more staff and issues being dealt with immediately, with quicker management decision-making. This is particularly important where one particular manager may travel to attend a meeting and return with a number of actions which in turn have to be dealt with by other people, involving further communication and time – through the medium of videoconferencing, this can be avoided.

Videoconferences take place via a live video connection. To enable the connection, the destination number (like a telephone number) is dialled to connect to another user, in the same way that a telephone call is made. The system itself is similar to a large television set, but it includes an integral camera and separate microphone. Different videoconferencing systems are available for various uses and these fall into three categories:

- *Studio-based systems*: these are the largest (and most expensive) systems and are frequently set up in a dedicated room. They are more usually found in multinational corporations that regularly communicate with large groups of people. Studio-based systems have options for additional cameras (e.g. document cameras), additional monitors and graphics transfer capability.
- *Rollabout systems:* these are smaller and can be moved from one room to another, allowing greater flexibility. They are usually the size of a large television set and also have options for additional cameras and facilities to link up with PCs to transfer data.
- *Desktop systems*: these are integrated into the desktop PC, which is fitted with a microphone and camera. The PC has special software installed to allow simultaneous exchange of voice, data and image. The advantages of a desktop system are enormous, with a number of people being able to 'meet' each other in their own working environment where they have everything they may need.

Recent packages go further than merely providing participants with the ability to see and hear each other. One of the greatest advantages, particularly with the desktop system, is the facility for all participants to share common information on the computer screen. For example, let us look at a meeting to discuss a new product design. You may have four PC windows running concurrently on the screen: in the first window you will have the audio and visual meeting in progress; the second window may display a graphics program detailing the design of the product in discussion; the third window may display a spreadsheet program with the various costings; and the fourth may have the word processing document outlining the specifications. Naturally, this enables all meeting participants to work together on a common project in their own environments, although they may physically be thousands of miles apart. Data sharing also means that meeting participants can work with a colleague's application remotely, even though it is not resident on their PCs. Real-time processing enables any of these windows to be updated on screen, with the change taking effect on all screens. This facility to share images and data is a vast benefit and provides an advantage not normally found in conventional meetings: it enables participants to 'bring' to a meeting any video, audio, graphic or text information they wish to share.

Recent enhancements to videoconferencing include:

- automatic conference scheduling and meeting notifications;
- the facility to have the computer take the minutes of the meeting, which can later be edited and transmitted electronically to all participants;
- a personal notepad on each desktop PC to allow individual participants to make personal notes during the meeting.

Obviously videoconferencing offers many advantages, with the main disadvantage being for the participant on the other side of the world who is obliged to get up in the middle of the night to take part in a video conference!

Scheduling a Meeting

It is usually the secretary who has responsibility for setting up meetings. Try to follow these guidelines, or make your own checklist to ensure that all requirements are met and that nothing has been forgotten.

Before the meeting is scheduled, you need to find out:

- who will host the meeting;
- the subject of the meeting;
- who needs to attend;
- how many attendees there will be;
- how long the meeting will take;
- where the meeting will be held;
- at what time it will start.

Once you have the answers to these questions, you can look at the actual logistics and start planning the meeting. This may involve very little or a lot of organization.

Begin by looking at the logistics.

- Size and location of meeting room required.
- Room arrangement: boardroom style for discussion, conference room style for presentations or classroom style for workshops.
- Number of chairs and tables required.
- Appropriate equipment: foil projectors, slide projectors, video recorders, televisions, flipcharts, pens, whiteboards, pinboards, computer equipment.
- Lighting and heating controls.
- Catering arrangements: jugs of water and cups on the tables, coffee available before the meeting and at break times, any sandwiches or working lunch arrangements.
- Stationery items: sufficient quantities of paper, pens, pencils, flipchart pens.
- Name cards or badges if appropriate.

Once the logistics have been planned and confirmed, the next step is the administrative work needed to set the meeting up.

- Send out a meeting advice to all required attendees, asking for confirmation of their attendance by a certain date if necessary, or any deputy or other attendee who may wish to come along.
- Invite any guest speakers who may be required to present. It is advisable to check their availability by telephone and to follow up with a written invitation. Once they have confirmed, you may wish to give them some information on the meeting attendees.
- Establish an agenda. This should include start and end times, scheduled breaks, times for individual presentations and names of speakers, details of meeting room and date. It is important to include times of breaks, as some participants may need to arrange telephone calls during the day and this can more effectively be done if they are aware of break times in advance.
- Ensure anyone who is playing an active part in the meeting – for example, hosting the meeting, taking the minutes, providing feedback or giving a presentation – is adequately briefed in advance.
- Send out a copy of the agenda to participants and speakers a few days in advance. It is a good idea to have additional copies available in the meeting room for those who have forgotten to bring their copy.
- Make sure the meeting 'host' is well prepared, knows who the key speakers are and is able to introduce them properly. He or she should also be aware of the catering arrangements and who to contact in case of problems, and should be responsible for keeping the meeting to time as far as possible.
- Ensure that all presentations are typed and prepared well in advance and that the appropriate audio-visual equipment is available.
- Arrange to get copies of all presentations beforehand. Photocopy these for the attendees and gather them into a folder to give each person at the close of the meeting. This ensures that each participant goes away with some information on the meeting.

MEETING ON AGENDA CONSTRUCTION
14 DECEMBER 1994
CONFERENCE ROOM ONE

09.00	Welcome and Introduction	Host
09.15	Minutes of Last Meeting	All
09.30	Presentation on xxxxxxxxx	Guest Speaker 1
10.30	Coffee	
10.45	Presentation on xxxxxxxxx	Guest Speaker 2
11.45	Open Discussion on xxxxxxx	All
12.30	Any Other Business	
12.45	Close and Lunch	

Figure 18 Example of an agenda.

Presentations

If you are given a presentation to prepare, you need to understand which medium the presenter plans to use. Several facilities are available, all with various benefits and drawbacks: for example, slide projectors, overhead projectors, video machines, Barco; to mention but a few. Probably the most used and easiest to prepare are foil presentations for an overhead projector.

If you are typing transparencies, always ensure you use a large print – there is nothing more frustrating for an audience (or a presenter) than presentation that cannot be well seen. Use a large typeface and a bold print to ensure maximum quality. Top and tail all your transparencies in a uniform way, giving details of the title of presentation, date and author. Try to maintain a consistent style throughout a presentation, using the same formats for headers, footers and bullets. Keep the number of words to a minimum, where possible using just bullet points.

If you type a lot of presentations, keep a log of them with the reference file number. Also keep a hardcopy version, as often certain presentations (e.g. organization or company goals) may be used many times, and it will save you the time and effort required in retyping. You may also care to remember that 'a picture speaks a thousand words', and this is particularly true in a presentation.

If you require slides or other material that will need to be prepared off-site, always remember to leave plenty of time for the printer to make the slides.

A meeting doesn't end when the last person leaves and the door is closed. Not only will the room need to be rearranged, checked over to find out if anyone has left anything behind and prepared for the next attendees, but the final part of the secretary's role needs to be completed.

You should send out 'thank you' letters to any guest speakers, expressing your manager's gratification and, where appropriate, including any positive feedback received from attendees. Minutes of the meeting should also be typed up as quickly as possible afterwards and sent to all attendees.

It may be the secretary's task to take the minutes of a meeting. If this is the case, always bear in mind that minutes are only intended as a brief record of what actually took place during the meeting, including any major decisions or objectives made.

Ensure you list the people who are attending, with titles and companies, if appropriate. Make a note of those people who would normally attend, but who have sent apologies. This is important where any decisions are taken, as a record needs to be maintained. Next follow with a brief description of each item discussed and any decision that was taken. Where action is to be taken, you should list the name of the person responsible and a due date for completion. Minutes should not be a lengthy and detailed report of everything that was said and done throughout the meeting. The last item of the minutes should give the arrangements and detail of the next meeting, if one is already scheduled. An example of some minutes is attached. Taking minutes is a skill that needs to be developed, so that you learn to note only the essential parts and avoid the unnecessary discussion.

Minutes of Departmental Meeting
15 February 1992

Present:	Joe Bloggs
	Fred Smith
	Bob Brown
	Sid Black
Apologies:	Simon Jones (holidays)

Item 1
This should be a brief resumé of the first item discussed.
ACTION: Name of person to action   **DUE DATE:** Date action needs to be taken

Item 2
As above and so on, giving each item an action and due date (as appropriate).
ACTION: Name of person to action   **DUE DATE:** Date action needs to be taken

Next meeting
Give details of the date, time and venue for the next meeting

_____

Signature of minute taker

Figure 19 Example of minutes layout.

Agendas and minutes should be kept in a folder pertaining to that particular meeting subject; these can then be easily found in preparation to take to the next meeting.

You may wish to consider composing a meeting evaluation sheet for attendees to mark on items such as administrative preparation, logistics, quality of room and equipment, efficiency of meeting notification and comments on presentations. This can be of particular value in assessing future meeting needs and in assisting you with meeting preparation.

Finally, remember that the planning of a meeting is as important as the meeting itself.

Organizing Events

Events can vary tremendously in both format and number of attendees. They can be anything from the departmental Christmas lunch to major product launches and press releases.

Many companies take advantage of promotional offerings to enhance business relationships and get to know people in a social sense, while benefiting in a commercial sense. For example, tennis at Wimbledon is a big company favourite. Tickets for the best matches are coveted and the large companies will frequently make their presence known with marquees and similar exhibitions. Other favourites are sports matches – rugby, cricket or golf. Considering that the majority of top business managers tend to be men, the sports arena is a very popular and civilized place to discuss business.

Other companies may use product launches and press releases as major customer events, to help their customers feel part of the company success.

The types of events and the methods of organization are far too numerous to go into detail here, but let us look at some of the various sorts of events and how we go about organizing these.

Christmas lunch

This is probably the simplest and most enjoyable event to organize. First, you need to ascertain how many people will be invited and how the event will be funded. This can alter your choice of venue considerably. If the employee is paying, you will need to look for a venue that will suit everyone's pockets. If the company is paying, you need to confirm the spending limit and ensure you get the best value for money.

Once these two primary factors have been confirmed, you should:

- Approach various restaurants, winebars, pubs and ask for samples of their Christmas menus and wine lists. Check to find out if they are doing any special entertainment for the Christmas season.
- Find a date that is convenient for everyone and ensure they are all aware of it well in advance.

- Once you have decided on a venue, you will need to give the restaurant plenty of advance notice of your choice of date and the numbers attending.
- Send a confirmation letter and deposit (if required) to the restaurant.
- Occasionally, you will find that menus need to be chosen a few days in advance. If this is the case, ensure you receive everyone's menu choice, notify the restaurant and keep a copy.
- You may wish to arrange a selection of drinks for when the guests arrive, prior to sitting down to eat. Talk to the restaurant staff and they will sort this out for you.
- Arrange a seating plan, if this is appropriate, and make up little placecards to put on the table.
- Find out whether crackers, party poppers, hats and novelties are provided. If not, check that the restaurant has no objection, and arrange to purchase, if appropriate.
- Always make sure that both you and the restaurant know how the bill will be paid on the day. It can be very embarrassing if no payment arrangements have been made in advance.
- Arrange to get to the restaurant half an hour earlier to check that everything is as you want it, to put placecards on the table and to confirm last minute arrangements with the restaurant manager.

Finally, if you are attending – enjoy yourself!

Promotional events

These are frequently handled by agencies, whose responsibility is to purchase tickets and arrange catering. Take, for example, a rugby match. An agency will purchase a block of tickets, which in turn will be 'sold' to a company as part of a package to include a marquee, drinks and food.

These sort of events can work out to be very expensive per head and therefore need careful planning to ensure the maximum benefit is obtained for the company. Your role will be to coordinate the requirements and liaise with the agency. Below is a list of some of the things you should look at.

- Number of attendees: you will usually be limited to a precise number and will want to ensure these places are filled, so have a reserve list. You need to make sure that you have a fair relative number of customers to employee hosts: a good ratio is to allow for four to five customers for every attending employee.
- Level of attendees. When inviting customers, it is imperative that you invite people of a similar level or rank so that no one feels offended at being with more junior or senior people.
- Once a list of customers has been drawn up, it is a good idea to invite them verbally to make sure it is in their diaries at the earliest opportunity, and to follow this with an invitation giving more detail. Always attach a response sheet, so that the customer can respond with any special requirements, such as dietary needs.

- Monitor responses closely. If an invitee declines, invite another customer as soon as possible. Remember, never invite people too late in the day, unless you know them very well – they may feel like an afterthought and this is bad for relationships.
- You may wish to send a follow-up letter a week or so before the event to confirm any arrangements such as time and meeting points. It is a good idea to include a telephone number, should they need to contact someone on the day of the event itself. Ask one of the employees to take a mobile phone and be responsible for the telephone messages. Always include any tickets that should be sent in advance, or a map.
- Ensure any requirements for accommodation, travel, parking, maps or dietary needs are taken care of in advance.
- Draw up a list of attendees, giving details of their position, company and anything else that may be of value to the host.
- Liaise at all times with the agency staff and ensure they are kept fully aware of what is happening.

Other events

Many events take place in the office: these could be press releases, products launches or exhibitions. Each event will have its own individual requirements and will therefore be different. Here again, good planning is imperative.

As a general guideline, you may like to consider the following:

- number of attendees;
- location of event;
- available media for exhibitions, presentations, etc.;
- layout of room(s);
- catering arrangements;
- timings of event;
- sufficient staff on hand to assist on the day;
- brochures, booklets or other company promotional material.

You will usually find that the number of attendees is never what you anticipate. There is usually quite a high drop-out rate for the larger events, but you will need to over-cater rather than run the risk of having insufficient food and drink available.

You will also need to make sure that the location is of a sufficient size and is insured for the number of attendees. Make sure that there are places for them to hang their coats, and enough seats around.

If you are organizing the layout of the event, try to keep the refreshments away from the main exhibition or presentation area, but set up on a number of smaller tables to encourage guests to circulate.

Whatever the event, the emphasis is on planning. Draw up a timetable well in advance and try to stick to it. For example:

Two months before:
- arrange location of event;
- check arrangements for presentations;
- organize any guest speakers;
- book the event in diaries of key personnel;
- publicize the event as appropriate.

Six weeks before:
- draw up a list of guests to invite;
- send out invitations;
- liaise with caterers regarding menus;
- organize a floor layout.

Four weeks before:
- monitor invitation responses;
- arrange for promotional materials;
- confirm with guest speakers.

Two weeks before:
- confirm numbers with caterers;
- confirm venue arrangements;
- draw up a final attendee list.

On the day:
- ensure host and employees are briefed;
- organize venue, food and exhibitions, according to your plan;
- arrange a visitor 'reception';
- exhibit promotional material.

This is only a brief guideline. Obviously, every event is different and therefore requires different organization and time scales, but you may find this timetable of some use in planning your events.

Information Technology in the Office

Over the past twenty years the machinery in offices has changed beyond all recognition. Gone are the manual typewriters, replaced by electric typewriters and subsequently by memory typewriters before the word processor took over. Most offices now have an amazing array of electronic equipment to enable them to function effectively and efficiently. Word processors, computers, fax machines, mobile telephones and all manner of advanced telecommunication methods combine to make communication very fast and very simple. Technology advances at an incredible speed, challenging the traditional roles in an organization, and this is particularly relevant to the secretary.

In many ways the job is much easier. There is no painstaking retyping of letters and documents when the boss changes his mind over a word: the word processor has provided the means for work to be changed quickly. It is far quicker to send a fax or an electronic message halfway across the world, knowing that it will arrive instantaneously without subjection to the vagaries of the mail. Yet this advanced technology requires a different skill set and a different kind of knowledge to operate the equipment required. The electronic office has meant that secretaries have to understand computers, how they function and how to make the best use of them for efficiency and job satisfaction.

The world of information technology is here to stay, and although the 'paperless office' remains a glint in a scientist's eye, the more we understand about computers the more effectively we can operate as secretaries.

What is a Computer?

A computer is an electronic machine that stores and processes data or information. Computers do not have brains, nor do they have the capacity to think for themselves. They are controlled automatically and work at very high speeds, which makes them extremely efficient and accurate. However, it is important to remember that the really valuable part of the work is done by the people who feed information into the computer and program it to carry out particular operations. Computers are logical machines which perform calculations, store vast volumes of information, transfer, sort and compare data.

The term 'computer' covers many different machines. As technology develops, computers become smaller and more powerful, and their uses expand and diversify. Often computers are designed specifically for a particular function: for example, you may have a machine that weighs the materials used in the construction of a product. Machines used in industry will have different specifications from those used in an office. We will look at various uses of the computer in different environments, but first it is important to understand how a computer works and the main parts of the machine.

Computers are not as new to the office as people imagine. Desktop calculators, the computer's early ancestors, have been around for many years: the first mechanical calculator was invented by Pascal as long ago as 1642! Although very little progress was made in developing this machine further, the first punch cards appeared in 1801 when a Frenchman called Jacquard invented a system for controlling the different threads on his weaving loom. These punch cards were developed further by Babbage and in 1833 the first automatic calculator appeared using punch cards. An American, Hollerith, further developed this system and in 1889 produced an electromagnetic calculating machine which was used until electronic computers were truly born in the aftermath of the Second World War.

In 1948, IBM introduced its Selective Sequence Electronic Calculator, which was the first operating computer to combine electronic computation and stored instructions. Technology began to make rapid developments, seemingly overnight, with medium-scale computers beginning to appear in businesses as early as 1954. Further advances in technology created greater compatibility and larger computers with an extensive variety of uses, and the computer became part of our everyday lives. In 1981, IBM introduced the revolutionary Personal Computer (PC), which created an overnight sensation and brought computing within everyone's reach. Portable computers were introduced in the 1980s: personal computers became smaller, first as 'laptops' which fitted neatly into briefcases and later as 'notebooks'. This means that even executives on the move can use their travelling time to deal with correspondence, analyse records, input information and stay in touch with the office.

Different Types of Computer

There are many different makes of computer but these can be divided into five main categories, each of different size and with a different target environment. These are:

Mainframe computers

These are very large computers which are generally accommodated in computer rooms that are specially constructed to maintain a constant temperature. These large boxes generate a lot of heat and air conditioning is essential to ensure they are kept cool and function as designed. Mainframe computers can have many different applications attached to them: for example, word processing packages or printers. They have a huge memory and work at a very fast speed, enabling a large volume of data to be input or output in a variety of ways. They are generally found in large organizations: for example, banks, airlines, oil industries or insurance companies.

Minicomputers

These are similar to mainframe computers, but are much smaller. Minicomputers are less temperamental than mainframes and do not require specially conditioned rooms. They cost less to run and so are a better alternative for a smaller organization, but they do not provide an appropriate environment for such a wide variety of applications or peripherals.

Microcomputers

These are smaller still, but this is the largest family of computers. Personal computers and desktop computers (which sit on your desk!) belong to the microcomputer family. They are smaller and need less space because the chips are developed to a different density and hold more information in a smaller space. Microcomputers allow the use of multitasking (working on more than one application concurrently: for example, word processing and accessing electronic mail at the same time). They can be 'intelligent' terminals which give the user independence as the PC possesses its own central processing unit (CPU), memory and disk storage. Or they can be 'dumb' terminals, which are completely dependent on the main PC's (server's) CPU and possess no processing power or memory of their own. PCs come with different processing speeds, which are determined by the processor type and the clock speed, which is measured in megahertz (MHz). Generally, the higher the speed, the faster the processing, so a computer running at 66 MHz is significantly slower than one running at 133 MHz, although the type of CPU and amount of memory (RAM) are also important. Microcomputers offer great variety and functionality and for these reasons are found in most organizations and businesses.

Laptops and notebooks

These are small personal computers which are designed to be completely mobile. They can be folded into themselves and open up in the same way as a briefcase or large book. They can run on battery power or mains power, making them a very suitable alternative for a mobile workforce (for example, sales people who are constantly out in the field and rarely in the office). They are also very efficient for people who travel frequently or for people working at home or other locations. Many of the

Information Technology in the Office

newer models of notebooks and laptops now have built-in modem cards to enable easy access to electronic mail and other on-line applications.

Personal organizers

These are pocket computers which are about the size of a small paperback book, weigh very little and fit in a pocket. They were primarily designed with facilities for an electronic diary and calculator, but the more advanced models offer the ability to compose memos and lists, and some have spreadsheet and word processing packages, or even handwriting recognition. They run on batteries. Some can interface with PCs to transfer data from the pocket computer to the PC.

How a Computer Works

Data is entered using an 'input device' (e.g. the keyboard). The information is transferred to the CPU, where it is processed. It can then be transferred to an 'output device' (e.g. a screen or printer). Linked to the CPU is the 'backing store' (the disk drive) where the information is stored. We will look at these various components in more detail, as they are all very important in understanding the computer.

From Figure 20 you can see how data moves around the various components of the computer. It can be transferred to the CPU and then printed and saved in the backing store. Data can also be brought out of storage and retrieved into the input buffer: for example, the computer screen. Now let us look at the functions of the CPU, as this is the control unit where most activity takes place.

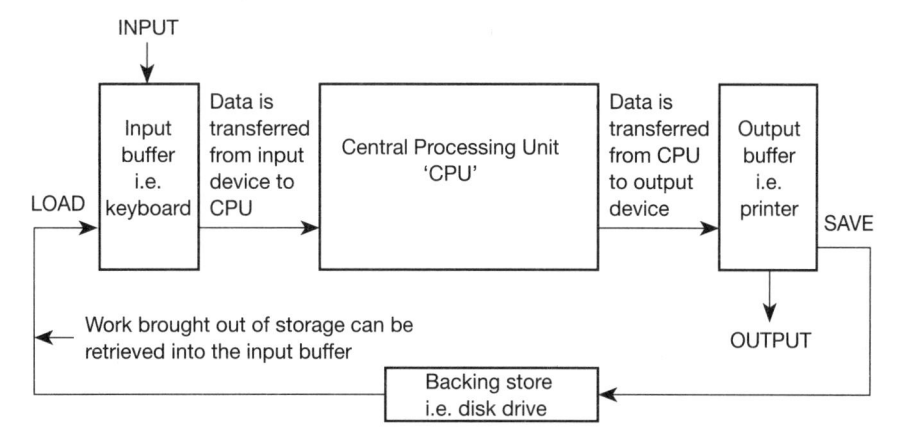

Figure 20 The components of a computer and how it works.

Central processing unit

The central processing unit consists of four main components and data flow continuously between the main units.

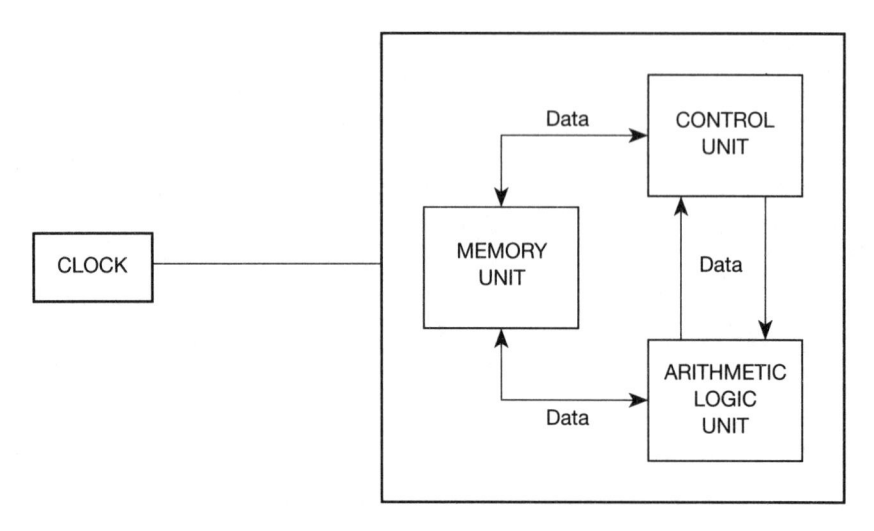

Figure 21 A central processing unit.

- The *control unit* is the nerve centre of the machine and is responsible for the running of the computer. It is like a set of traffic lights that controls the movement of data.
- The *arithmetic logic unit* is where all the calculations and analyses are performed.
- The *memory unit* is where the information is held until it is needed or transferred to the backing store. The memory can be a volatile unit and it is best to transfer data to the backing store regularly to prevent any loss.
- The *clock* sends out pulses at a fixed rate, e.g. 10 million pulses per second. These pulses are the means by which the control unit synchronizes all the system's actions.

Input Devices

Input devices provide the method of entering data into the computer. There are several ways of inputting information into the system, although probably the most common method is the keyboard, particularly in an office environment.

- *Keyboard*: the most common input device, which was invented in 1873 and is known in the UK as the QWERTY keyboard (from the first row of letters). Most are alphanumeric, with programmable function keys. It is worth noting that the arrangement of keyboards is not universal and the position of letters varies according to the country.

Information Technology in the Office

- *Mouse*: this is a small device usually attached to the end of a lead which is plugged into the computer. It manipulates the cursor in a similar way to the cursor keys on a keyboard and enables the user to move around the screen. The two buttons on the mouse have different functions. Mice are becoming a standard device for entering text, particularly in a Microsoft Windows environment.
- *Punch cards*: these are seldom found in the office now, although they used to be the traditional way of inputting information. The cards were punched with a pattern of holes corresponding to a binary code. The advantage of using punchcards was the opportunity to prepare input material away from the computer. They were frequently used for batch processing applications, such as salary runs
- *OCR or optical character recognition*: a method of scanning each character and converting it into a pattern of electronic signals. OCR readers can recognize over 300 different fonts, read up to 200 pages per hour and have a low error rate. The main advantage is enabling correspondence to be scanned in and avoiding the repetition of typewritten work. Some organizations scan customer correspondence into the system for electronic filing purposes.
- *Badge card readers*: these are frequently used for credit cards, security passes and ATM (automatic teller machine – cashpoint) cards. The information is securely maintained on a magnetic strip on a plastic card.
- *Optical wands*: otherwise known as light pens, these read the information on a bar code. They are frequently found at supermarket checkouts where the pricing and stock information is held in the bar code. Another method using the same technique is the laser scanner contained in a desk over which the object is passed to read the information.
- *Voice input*: this is a very new area which involves speaking into a microphone attached to the computer, which converts the spoken word into written text. This is now available as a dictating method for office work and could revolutionize the working environment, particularly for secretaries. Security passwords could be incorporated into voice patterns instead of key strokes.
- *Touch sensitive screens*: these are special screens which have icons that can be touched to produce information as requested. These are becoming familiar in public places, where they give more information about available attractions.
- *Pen input*: this is a relatively new method of inputting text or diagrams into a palmtop computer by means of a special light pen with which the text is added to the screen. The information inputted can be stored on the palmtop and later uploaded on to a PC if required. With some models, the handwritten text can be reformatted into typewritten face.

There are many other, less common, input devices, but these tend to be more specialized, and developed for more specific organizations or industries.

Output Devices

Output devices provide a way of converting stored information into a version that we can easily understand. By far the most common method is printing and there are several different varieties of printer to suit different requirements. Before we look at the various printers, let us examine the other output devices you will find in the office.

- *VDU (visual display unit)*: this is the screen or the monitor of your computer. The data you input via the mouse or the keyboard appear on the screen in a readable format, in the same way that the letters of a typewriter keyboard appear on a piece of paper. A monitor is like a television screen with produces images through dots. The higher the resolution (greater density of dots), the clearer the picture on your screen. Monitors come in various sizes, although the most common size is probably a 14 inch screen. They also come in colour, or in black and white (known as mono), although colour screens are far more usual now.
- *Microfiche or microfilm*: these are more frequently found in libraries than in offices. Microfiche is film on which the computer photographs documents and this film can be viewed through certain projectors.
- *Video output*: CD-ROM is not only a method of storage but a way of distributing material in multimedia. Information is complete with sound effects, words and pictures, and this is particularly useful for teaching children, with many books and encyclopaedias becoming available in CD-ROM format. A simple example of this is the word 'clock': this would bring up a picture of a clock, a word description and a ticking sound.
- *Barco*: this is used in conferences and presentations and is basically a projector which projects the presentation material from a PC directly on to a large screen. The user can move between slides and presentations by using the keyboard or mouse of the PC, while the audience views only the charts on the screen.
- *Voice output*: some computers are equipped with a 'voice' which is programmed to produce pre-recorded words. Examples are a lift which talks its way through the floors or certain toys that can interpret sounds, like a talking parrot that will reiterate the words someone has just spoken.

Printers

There are many different types of printer available, varying from the very large, very fast printers found in a copying shop or print-room of a large organization, to small printers which will fit into a briefcase with a notebook computer. Basically they can be divided into two main groups: *impact printers*, which produce an image by applying pressure against a ribbon in the same way as a typewriter works; and *non-impact printers*, which output material without applying any pressure on the paper. These are the main printers you will find in the office:

Information Technology in the Office

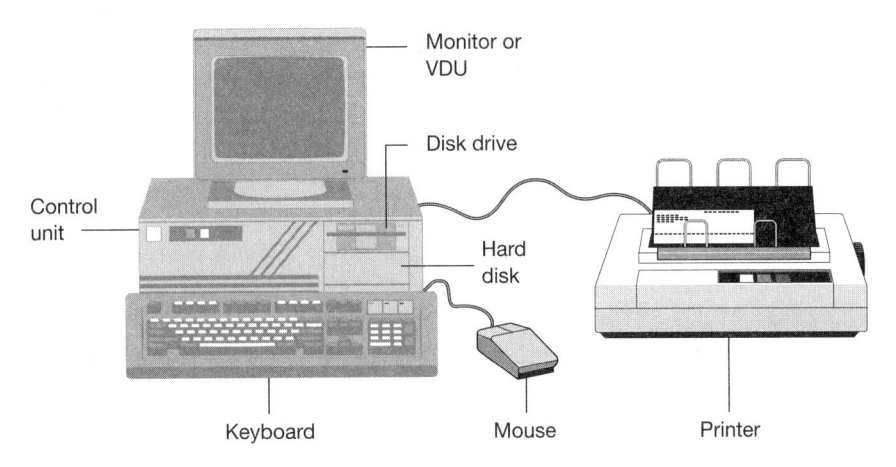

Figure 22 Components of a personal computer.

- *Daisy wheel printer*: this is an impact printer with the characters stamped on a daisy wheel, i.e. a small wheel with many protruding fingers on which the characters are imprinted: it is the wheel with these many 'petals' that gave it its name. The wheel can spin quickly in either direction and can move along the page in both directions. As it moves it stamps the characters on the paper. It is a very high quality printer offering different fonts and pitches.
- *Dot-matrix printer*: this is a much cheaper printer and is frequently used for home work or for draft copies in an office. It works by creating an image from a number of dots. These dots are formed by a row of pins which hammer against a ribbon to produce the characters on the paper. The greater the number of pins, the higher the quality of printing, as the dots appear closer together to give it a more fluent outline. The most common dot-matrix printers are 9-pin and 24-pin, with the 24-pin being the more efficient printer.
- *Plotter*: this is a very slow printer which prints in colour by controlling a number of small coloured felt-tip pens that pass over the paper systematically and draw the image. It is occasionally used for presentations in offices (although colour laser printers have now largely taken over). However, plotters are frequently used in the engineering industry.
- *Line printer*: these impact printers are only suitable for use with a system that requires speed and not quality. They print in lines and can produce between 200 and 2,000 lines per minute. They are most frequently used for computer-generated reports.
- *Thermal printer*: this is a non-impact printer which creates an image in a similar way to a dot-matrix printer, with the exception that the print is generated by heat against special (thermal) paper. This is quick and reliable, but these printers are not frequently used because of the expense of special paper.
- *Inkjet printer*: this is a non-impact printer which produces the characters by forcing ink on to the paper in a stream of ink drops to form the required charac-

ters. There is no ribbon, but a small ink cartridge which is easily replaced. Inkjet printers (or bubblejet printers as they are also known) are quiet, efficient and quick, with the facility to print graphics as well as letters, and are therefore widely used in the home and office. They now come in a compact size which fits easily into a briefcase with a notebook computer providing complete independence and mobility. Colour inkjets are widely available and inexpensive.

- *Laser printer*: this is a very fast non-impact printer and very often found in the office. It creates the image in much the same way as a photocopier. It produces excellent quality and works at a very high speed. It offers a lot of versatility, as it can reproduce graphics and text in a variety of fonts, sizes and styles. Many laser printers have their own memory built in. Colour laser printers are also available to produce graphics and text in different colours and these are particularly useful for presentation transparencies.

In addition to the various types of printer available, there are different options for feeding the paper into the printer. These are:

- *Continuous feed*: here the paper is contained in a tray which will usually hold between 50 (for smaller inkjets) and 500 (for large lasers) sheets, and the paper is fed continuously into the printer as it is required.
- *Sheet feed*: this requires the individual sheets of paper to be fed into the printer by hand. This is an option usually chosen when special paper or letterhead paper is being used.
- *Tractor feed*: this again is a continuous paper feed, but here each sheet of paper is attached to the next with perforated dots. There is a series of holes down the sides of the paper designed to fit the tractor feed, enabling the printer to hold the paper in position while it prints. A tractor feed is two wheels fitted to either end of the roller, each wheel having about ten large spikes over which the paper slots. This type of paper feed is usually used for printing large volumes of forms, or, for example, on a payroll system where salary details are printed on to pre-printed forms.

Storage

It is essential to save all your work and to make back-up copies frequently. Computers are not infallible and occasionally crash – taking your hard work with them. As you process information it is stored in the memory unit of the CPU, but must then be transferred to a more permanent storage area. Backing storage is the term given to saving material away from the CPU and there are several ways of storing information.

- *Hard disks*: these are magnetic disks made of a strong, rigid material which are nearly always stored in the body of the PC and are not therefore easily handled or damaged. The size of the hard disk varies according to the size of the machine. It is usually used to store the software programs that are accessed regularly and the information produced is then stored on diskette. Data on hard disks can be accessed much more quickly than that on diskettes.

- *Diskettes* are the most frequently used medium for saving information. They are used mainly by microcomputers and are made of flexible plastic coated with iron oxide, and then encased. Most are double-sided and high density. They are usually available in two sizes. The 3.5 inch diskette is the smaller of the two and tends to be of a more rigid plastic. It is also the most commonly found. It usually stores 1.44 Mb of information. The 5.25 inch floppy diskette is a larger, more flexible diskette which is usually found in older PCs. It usually stores 1.2 Mb of information. A diskette stores information on its surface within a number of tracks (usually 80 tracks). Before you can store information on a new diskette, you may need to format it to enable information to be stored in a retrievable way. All diskettes must be handled very carefully to prevent damage (some hints on looking after your diskettes are given below). You can protect the information on your diskette by using the protect option – on the 3.5 inch diskette this is a small piece of plastic which you can slide to open: once it is opened the disk can be read but not stored to. If you want to store or change it once it has been protected, you will need to slide the small plastic piece back.
- *Compact disks (CDs)* are rigid circular disks which use laser light technology to store data. They have a large capacity and are not so easily damaged as the magnetic diskettes. They come in a number of formats of which CD-ROM (Compact Disk-Read Only Memory) is probably the most well known. In the past it was not possible for office users to save material on CDs, and they were used only for distribution of software packages. However, CD-ROM writers are becoming more and more available.
- *Others*: tape streamers (similar to cassette recorders) have been used for a number of years to back-up the material on hard disks. Large capacity diskettes (some capable of storing 2,048 Mb) are now widely available for back-up purposes.

Looking after your disks is extremely important as the retrieval of your information is dependent on the state of the disk. Once a disk has been corrupted or damaged the information stored is irretrievable. *Always* take a back-up copy of information and take care of your diskettes by:

- never leaving them in the machine;
- putting them away in a diskette box at the end of use;
- never stapling or clipping a diskette to anything (put it in an envelope first to protect it);
- writing clearly but gently on the label so you know what is stored on the diskette;
- never leaving them exposed to heat or sunlight;
- never forcing a disk into a machine;
- never placing heavy objects on them or using them as a coaster for your coffee mug;

- never exposing them to the X-ray machines at airports;
- not touching the magnetic surface;
- never lending them to someone else (without taking a copy first).

There is nothing more frustrating than to lose the information you have spent hours creating because you have not saved the data, or because the disk is corrupted and the data cannot be retrieved. Taking care of your diskettes and ensuring you always take a copy of your material can go a long way towards ensuring you don't have to re-key any data.

Networks

Networks are used to link a number of computers together so that they can communicate with each other and share common software. In all networks there is a main computer called the 'file server' to which all the other terminals are linked by cables. The file server is an ordinary computer or PC which is the host because all the files used by the other computers are located on its hard disk. Networks are very common in large organizations using electronic mail. There are two kinds of networks.

- *Local area network (LAN):* this is used to link a number of computers located on the same premises. It is basically a single cable which runs through the office and has connections for the other computers or printers to be linked to the network. Usually all the software packages are held on the file server and accessed by each individual PC. Users must have authority to access the LAN and will have their own user ID and password with which they can access the LAN from any computer that is linked to it – it does not have to be the one they usually use. LANs have the advantage of being able to link terminals to the network whenever required. The main disadvantage of a LAN is that when the file server crashes all the other PCs crash too, and any information being processed is lost – although this should be a fairly rare occurrence.
- *Wide area network (WAN):* This is a network linked via the telecommunications networks, enabling terminals at different locations to be connected. Several LANs can be linked together in this way, giving the opportunity to benefit from both a local network and a wide area network. This is particularly advantageous to companies located in several towns and using an electronic mail facility.

From Figures 23 and 24 you can see the main difference between a local area network, which is located on one site only, and a wide area network, which allows communication between several sites via the telecommunications network, i.e. via telephone cables and satellite.

Both LANs and WANs are built along the same principle with a central file server, and it is as easy to transmit data around the country as it is to send information around the office.

Information Technology in the Office

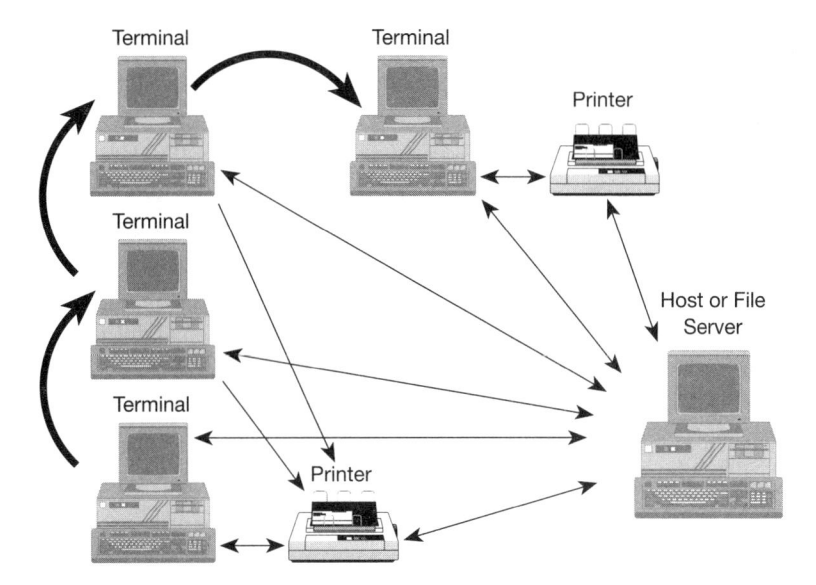

Figure 23 Local area network (LAN).

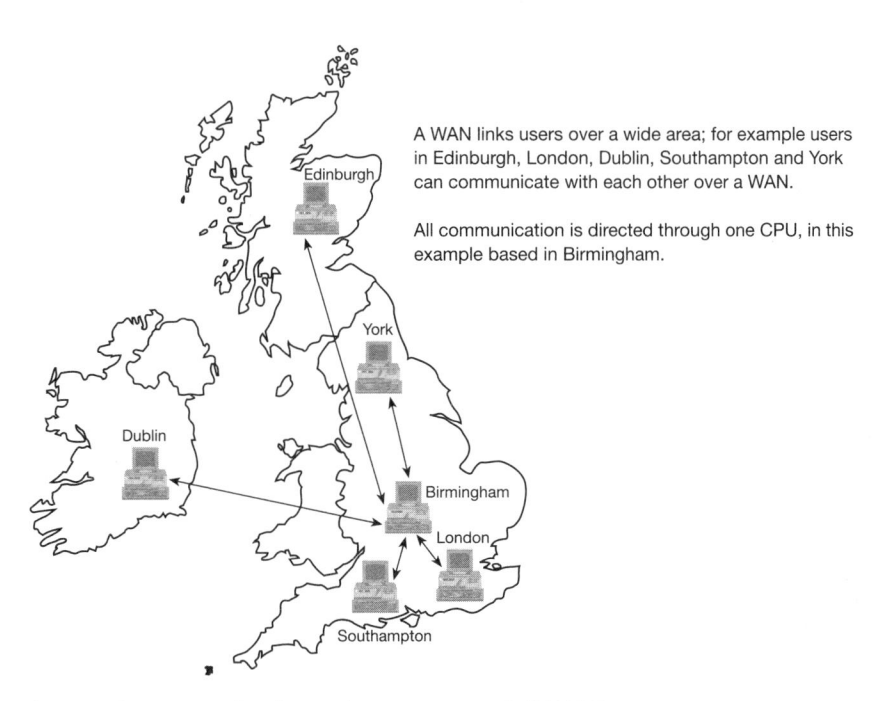

A WAN links users over a wide area; for example users in Edinburgh, London, Dublin, Southampton and York can communicate with each other over a WAN.

All communication is directed through one CPU, in this example based in Birmingham.

Figure 24 Example of a wide area network (WAN).

The main advantages of a network system are:

- the facility to communicate with each other;
- shared software application packages;
- ability to connect to a variety of printers;
- access to your own files from any terminal linked to the network, even if you are located in a different site office.

The main disadvantages are:

- when a file server crashes all the terminals crash too, and any information being processed is lost;
- file security can be a problem if the system is not properly password protected;
- some applications run more slowly on a network than on a standalone PC.

In addition to LANs and WANs there is the Internet, which is an international network to which anyone possessing a PC, modem, appropriate software and telephone line can be linked for a charge. This enables electronic communication with anyone in the world via computers and means you can send messages and documents to anyone else on the Internet. In addition, a lot of information is available for access.

Electronic Communication

Today it is just as easy to send electronic mail to someone at the next desk, in the next town or the other side of the world! Electronic mail (e-mail) is becoming more and more common in businesses of all sizes and many organizations have their own e-mail systems. In addition to sending notes to each other, many systems offer the facility to attach documents created in word processing, graphics or spreadsheet packages to the note. These are sent as an attachment which can then be downloaded and formatted at the destination address.

To communicate with each other, each user needs to have access to a network. This means that information can be sent over telephone cables and satellites to reach the destination. Each e-mail user has his own 'userid' or 'address': this is his own personal address, which ensures that mail arrives at the correct place, rather like hardcopy mail being sent to our home address. Notes are sent over the networks, which means they may arrive instantaneously or they may take longer. It depends on the state of the network and whether there are hold-ups of any kind: for example, a telephone line may be down.

In addition to mail, it is possible to send faxes directly from a terminal to a fax machine. This means we simply type the information we want to fax into our terminal as a normal note or document and the message is sent via the network to the destination fax machine where it prints as a normal fax.

To access your e-mail you need to sign into your own system. All mail systems are password protected to ensure security, and you will be prompted to ask for your elec-

Information Technology in the Office

tronic sign-on, followed by your password, before you are given access to your mailbox. Once you can access your mailbox, you will probably have several options and can choose to deal with your notes in different ways: read, print, forward to someone else, reply to the sender, file or delete. The range of options depends on the e-mail system you are using.

There are many advantages to an e-mail system:

- communication with other people both inside and outside your company;
- ability to access mail at any time and from any location (even from home with the appropriate equipment);
- fast, efficient distribution of mail worldwide – no time spent in the post;
- no paper, photocopying or postage costs, although there are the obvious costs of telecommunications;
- an electronic record of all outgoing and incoming correspondence;
- facility to send faxes without having to print and send via the fax machine.

The disadvantages are few, although the main concern is security and access by unauthorized users.

The process between you sending your mail message and the recipient receiving it is extremely complex. First your note is passed along the cable to your file server and from there along telephone lines and via satellites where necessary to the destination server, where the note is then transmitted to the correct destination address via cables.

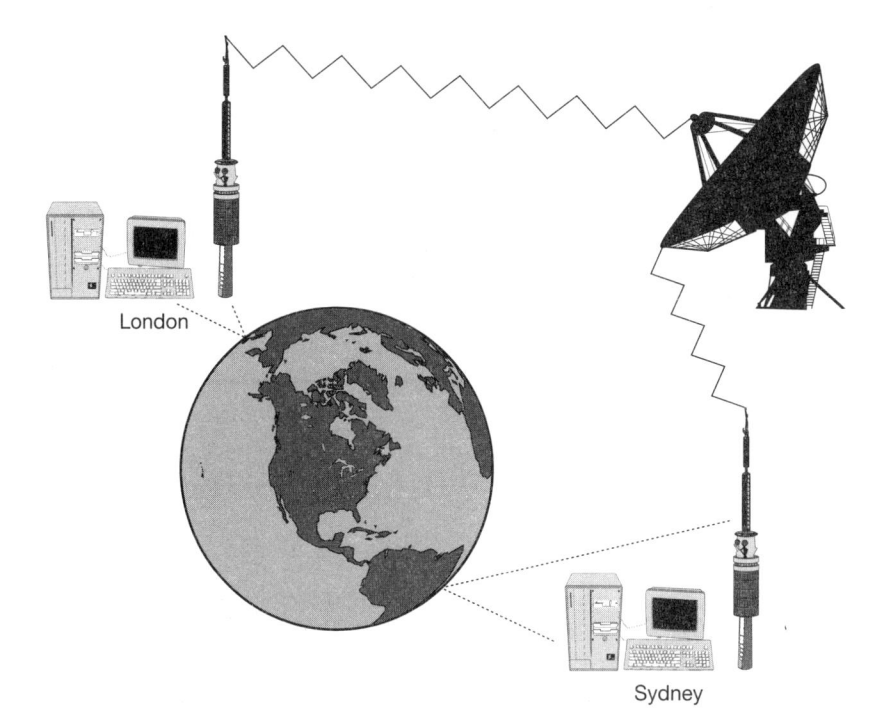

Figure 25 Journey of an electronic mail message.

Figure 25 shows the route your message would take if you were sending it from London to someone based in Sydney.

Security

With so much electronic communication and transmission of data around the world, security has become even more important. For those with sufficient knowledge to hack into a computer, the challenge is irresistible. Whether they are after specific information or simply wish to corrupt a system, it can cost an organization a fortune and computer fraud is on the increase.

We can help with simple security measures to protect our own data. By applying these procedures in our working environment, we are looking after our information.

- Never let anyone else use your system or access your files, particularly if he or she is not someone you work with.
- Only use the system for which you are authorized. Never use other people's systems.
- Don't be tempted by pirate software – often it contains viruses which can corrupt all your data files, and if you are linked to a network, it can corrupt your co-workers' data too.
- Look after your disks: keep them in a locked box in a locked cupboard.
- Don't give your password out to anyone else. Change your password regularly and if documents are extra-sensitive use a dual-password protection, particularly if they are stored on a network.

It is very important that your computer and your work are protected from viruses. A virus is a program that can infect and corrupt your software and data. They are usually spread through other people's diskettes or installing pirate software, although many are active on the Internet. Viruses can do many things: for example, display a message on your screen, erase your files, scramble information on your hard disk or use large amounts of disk space. Many are specifically designed by practical jokers to become active on 1 April or Friday the Thirteenth. To help protect against viruses, it is advisable to install a virus scanning program which will indicate if a virus is present and try to remove it.

To help with the prevention of computer fraud, the UK government passed two laws to protect both individuals and companies.

The Computer Misuse Act

This act was introduced in 1990 to help to alleviate the threats of hacking into computers and viruses. It is now a criminal offence, which can be punished by imprisonment for any term up to five years, for any individual to:

- access a computer system without the correct level of authority and intentionally exceeding the bounds of this authority;
- access a computer with the intention of committing a serious crime (for example, hacking into a system to embezzle funds from a bank account);
- change computer information, e.g. programs, without authority or use unauthorized software which may contain a virus.

The Data Protection Act

This is particularly important for secretaries, as frequently they are responsible for creating and maintaining personnel files on the system. The Data Protection Act was passed in 1984 to protect individuals whose details are kept on computer. The secretary (or appropriate person responsible) must ensure that data are lawful and adequate for the purpose required, that they are not kept any longer than necessary and that they are stored in a way that denies unauthorized access.

The Data Protection Registrar is a government body whose responsibility is to ensure that these rules are being adhered to. Individuals have the right to see information about them that is stored on computer at any time, and can legally claim compensation if they believe the information is wrong or unnecessary in any way.

What is Software?

Computers run on hardware and software. We know that hardware is the actual machine, printer, cables and all the peripherals that combine to make a computer work. But without software the computer will not run. Software is a program or a set of programs designed to give instructions that the processing unit understands and implements, so that the user can access the required functions. The program is simply a set of instructions written in a format that the computer understands.

We think of software in two ways. First, it is the operating system which provides an environment for packages to run: for example, Microsoft Windows is an operating system which allows us to run either Windows applications (e.g. Lotus AmiPro) or MS-DOS based packages (e.g. WordPerfect 5.1). The operating system loads the programs, activates them and controls them as they run. Second, applications packages are software programs, like word processing packages or spreadsheets. Software can be standard, and bought 'off the shelf', or can be 'bespoke', i.e specialist software written to a customer's specification. Standard packaged software can be tailored to meet a specific organizational need: for example, the air ticketing operation used by travel agents.

As a secretary, you are principally concerned with word processing packages, although it may help to know a little about some of the other available options which we may be required to use: for example, spreadsheet, database, presentation and desktop publishing packages.

Word Processing

There are many word processing packages available on the market today. The GUI (graphic user interface) versions – for example, those running on Windows – are becoming more standard. They are very easy to use.

Windows products use icons (little picture boxes) to perform most functions – for example, printing or saving – instead of using the function keys, and to access any function you would simply use the mouse button to click on the icon. The GUI makes word processing much easier, as what you see on the screen is how it will appear on paper. There are many packages available and still more are being developed, each offering more facilities and greater ease of use than the previous one.

However, some packages, such as Wordperfect 5.1, run on the MS-DOS (or PC-DOS) operating system and function keys are used to implement different effects in the same way that icons are used in Windows.

Function keys are the 'F' keys located on the keyboard and are used to perform certain operations: for example, F7 may be used to print a document. The functions attached to each key tend to differ between each package, and it is advisable to obtain and use an overlay giving a legend for the function keys.

Whichever you use, all word processing packages offer the following facilities, which are a vast improvement over the typewriter.

- Formatting text to ensure the document is properly laid out. This include facilities to underline, highlight, italicize, change font and size of text, justify text in various ways, alter the spacing, change the margins, add headers and footers to documents, force page breaks and automatically number pages.
- Text editing to facilitate restructuring text: copying, pasting, moving, deleting and changing text around in large chunks.
- Merge files which combine address files and documents to handle mailshots quickly without having to type each individual letter.
- A spellcheck facility to check the spelling of your document: most offer the option of your own customized dictionary so that you can add words or names that you use frequently.
- The facility to create and edit tables within your text.
- Printing options to format how your page will print and to send your printing to different printers according to the document: for example, you may want to print in colour.

In addition to these common functions, many packages also offer the following.

- Grammar checks and thesaurus assistance.

Information Technology in the Office

- The facility to insert graphics or pictures, either drawn within the word processing package or imported.
- The ability to import documents or parts of documents from other software programs: for example, importing a spreadsheet into a word processor. In the same way you can export your data to other programs.
- Table of contents and indexing facilities which automatically create a table of contents for your document, inserting page numbers, etc.
- Style sheets that allow you to choose your document format before you begin working: for example, a standard memo format or a fax header.
- Forms that are already on the system and for which you only need to complete the relevant fields.

It is very much a matter of personal preference which word processing package you or your company chooses, but most packages today are extremely efficient and greatly assist the secretary.

Spreadsheets

A spreadsheet is an electronic system used to record information and perform both simple and complex calculations quickly and efficiently. A spreadsheet package enables you to do all sorts of calculations very easily through the use of formulae. Information is entered into a screen that looks like a large form with many boxes. An example of a blank spreadsheet is given in Figure 26.

A spreadsheet can be composed of as many rows or boxes as required and these boxes, called 'cells', can be changed in width to accommodate data. Each of the cells has its own address and these are vital for performing calculations. The address is taken from the intersection of the column and row: for example, cell C2 is where row 2 meets column C.

Information entered into the cells can be formatted in different ways: for example, you may have a list of prices and want a currency denomination to appear, so you could choose the '£' option and select your decimal places to one or two places as you wish.

	A	B	C	D	E	F	G	H	I	J	K	L	M	N
1										J1				
2			C2											
3						F3								
4														

Figure 26 Example of part of a blank spreadsheet.

The great advantage of spreadsheets is that they do the calculations for you – once you have entered the formula. The formula is the instruction given for the calculation: for example, if you wanted to add all the numbers in column B, you would enter a formula in the cell at the bottom of the column which would tell the system to add all the numbers from B1 to B10 (or wherever your cursor is). In the same way that you can copy data in word processing, you can copy numbers or formulae in a spreadsheet package to save time.

Each spreadsheet package has its own way of entering formulae, but these basically use the mathematical signs that we all know, such as

- + addition
- − subtraction
- * multiplication
- / division
- = equals

Spreadsheets have many uses in the office environment. For example:

- maintaining departmental budgets;
- updating holiday records for personnel;
- availability reports for merchandise held in stock;
- log of orders in and orders out with values and running totals;
- forecasting and recording sales;
- keeping a skills record of personnel;
- cost analyses for work or services.

Many spreadsheet packages also offer the facility to show the information in a graph format, which can be very useful for incorporation into presentations or documents.

Databases

A database is like a glorified electronic filing system. It stores all the information required and enables you to sort and analyse information quickly and efficiently. For example, you can sort information alphabetically, numerically or by type.

A database structure is created before any information is entered and it is built in the same way that you may compose a form, i.e. by deciding which 'fields' you wish to use to store and later analyse your information. A 'field' is the generic name for the information you are entering. A 'record' is a completed set of fields: for example, information giving name, address, telephone number, etc. for one person. There is no limit to the number of records you may input. For example, you may choose fields that include name, age, address, etc. It is totally dependent on the sort of information you intend to enter into the database and how you plan to use it.

It is important to remember that the database is only as efficient as the information that is keyed in, and therefore input must be correct and consistent if it is to be of any value.

There are many uses for a database in the office.

- Customer profile databases would include details of all your customer information by name, title, company, address, telephone number, fax number, secretary's name and any other relevant information.
- Company information databases are very common in large organizations. These contain information which needs to be accessed by employees regularly and which must be kept up to date. A central database removes the need for frequent paper updates and can be quickly brought up to date. Information contained may include purchasing policies, expense guidelines, travel booking arrangements, holiday policy, sickness guidelines, company policies, dates of important events.
- Access databases for entry to secure areas protected by badge locks on doors. The database would give details of approved personnel, employee number and level of authority; this information would also be stored in the magnetic strip of the employee's badge, which would be read by the computer and checked against the database before entry was granted.
- Address book information, which could then be used for mail merges and would include details of name, title, company and address.
- On-line telephone directory for large organizations to enable an employee to find out the telephone number of another employee by entering the name and bringing up the information on that person. For example, it would include name, position, department, telephone number and location (or any other relevant information). A good example of this is the database used by Directory Enquiries when a caller rings to find the telephone number of a certain person or a particular company. When the information is entered the database brings up the entries which match the name. If there is more than one entry, further information fields (i.e. address) are used to find the correct number.
- Meetings or events calendars which would give details of the date, venue and subject of meetings.

Presentation Packages

Presentation packages are available for the express use of preparing presentations. They provide an environment for creating slides, transparencies and on-line presentations with the use of text, wordart and clipart.

Text is entered using the same method as a word processing package and can be formatted in many ways, with different fonts and sizes. Generally the size of the text is greater than that for documents so that the text can be clearly visible during the presentation.

Wordart is the term given to text that flows in a different format: for example, in an arc or circle or in the shape of an arrow. Clipart is the term given to designs which are already 'drawn' in the graphics system and can be retrieved from storage and inserted into a document. Packages today offer a great variety of wordart and clipart, with hundreds of designs to choose from to enliven a presentation.

In addition to the clipart, there are a variety of shapes you can import to compose your own diagrams, you can draw lines, arcs or arrows, boxes, circles or triangles, changing the colour, width and size to suit your chart. Alternatively, you can choose the freelance option, which allows you to draw freehand using the mouse as your electronic pencil – this is not easy!

Transparencies and charts created through presentation packages can be printed on laser or colour printers, although you need to check that there is sufficient memory available in the printer as graphics tend to occupy a lot of space.

Most presentation packages are Windows based now. Your page will be your slide or transparency and you can choose to compose it as you wish, using the icons to insert text, clipart or wordart. You can insert tables or compose graphs from data you have entered into tables.

Most packages offer 'page layouts', which give you a choice of various styles: for example, you may choose to begin with a 'title page' which gives you the space to enter your title and sub-title; you may then choose a 'bullet' layout on which to enter your title and a number of bullets. Other choices include graphs, tables or combinations.

In addition to the layouts, many packages offer different 'style sheets', which provide a choice of various backgrounds. This gives you the option of choosing a background relevant to the presentation you are creating. For example, you may choose a background showing a map of the world if your presentation centres on global operations. Or you may choose a background of different currencies if your subject is financial.

Graphics can also be imported into word processing documents, giving you the opportunity to insert relevant graphs, cartoons or pictures into your reports. Presentation programs are quite simple to learn and a lot of fun to use.

Desktop Publishing

Desktop publishing (DTP) packages offer many of the same facilities as the word processing packages on the market today. The main function of a DTP package is to prepare the text in a layout suitable for magazines or books. It is a useful package for composing newsletters or any sort of publication that requires a professional touch.

The DTP package contains instructions for 'typesetting' the document ready for publishing. It does this by bringing in the document text from a word processing package and applying to it a set of pre-designed instructions to specify typeface, style and size of letter, word and line spacing, text alignments, margins, columns and lines. It then lays out the text on the page according to these instructions.

Illustrations or graphs can be inserted at any point and text will flow around them automatically. Material like photographs or maps can be scanned into the document in electronic form if required. Headers, footers and page numbers are added to the document and it can be viewed on the screen in its end-result format.

Once the operator is satisfied with the appearance of the document a final printed version is produced and run off on a laser printer.

Acronyms, Abbreviations and Terminology

Computer language is rampant with acronyms, abbreviations and different terminology. Below are a few that you may come across and which you may find useful:

CAD/CAM	computer-aided design/computer-aided manufacturing
CD-I	compact disk-interactive
CD-ROM	compact disk-read only memory
DOS	disk operating system
DPI	dots per inch
GUI	graphic user interface
LAN	local area network
LQ	letter quality
LSI	large scale integration
Mb	megabyte (approximately 1 million bytes)
MHz	megahertz
NLQ	near letter quality (of printers)
OCR	optical character recognition
PC	personal computer
RAM	random access memory
VDU	visual display unit
WAN	wide area network
WIMPS	windows, icons, mouse, pointer
WYSIWYG	what you see is what you get

batch processing	information processed in large batches (e.g. payroll)
multi-tasking	running several tasks simultaneously
off-line processing	information prepared away from the computer
on-line processing	information processed on the computer
real-time processing	processing done straight away

Simple Accounting

Most people think of accounting as being a complex aspect of the business world best left to the professionals. However, it helps to understand the fundamentals of accounting and how to read and evaluate simple accounts such as profit and loss. Often a secretary may be asked to keep a departmental budget for all expenditure, she may be responsible for the petty cash, or she may be asked to reconcile expense accounts. It is therefore helpful to understand a little more about accounting principles to make your role easier and more interesting.

In basic terms, accounting is simply the recording of business transactions: the sales and payments for both goods and services, which are in turn used to evaluate and communicate the results of past records and to assist with business planning for the future. A more familiar term is bookkeeping, as records were originally maintained in ledgers or books and, although these are now usually computerized, they are still referred to as ledgers. Bookkeeping can be traced back many centuries: Egyptians used to record their business transactions in hieroglyphics, the Romans used to register their dealings in Latin. Today bookkeeping tends to take the form of 'double-entry' accounts, as each transaction has a two-fold effect on the business.

A small organization may only have one ledger for all its accounts, although as the organization grows so do the bookkeeping entries and a different system would be needed in time. Larger organizations require a different method and one that is easily understood and managed by more than one bookkeeper or accountant. The most efficient and usual way of organizing the accounts would be to maintain four ledgers.

- *Sales ledger*: containing all the customers' personal accounts with records of all sales of merchandise made.
- *Purchase ledger (or bought ledger)*: maintaining all records of suppliers' accounts, with information of products or services bought for the business.
- *Cash book*: registering all expenses paid out and receipts paid in cash or cheque. This may also constitute the petty cash book.
- *General ledger (or nominal ledger)*: containing any remaining accounts, and used most frequently to record all other accounts for assets, expenses, income, etc.

Glossary of Accounting Terms

Term	Definition
accounting period	a period of time used to measure and identify revenue and expenses: for example, it may be a quarter or a year
assets	possessions or property of some use and value to the business and which are wholly owned by the company
capital	the sum initially invested in the business; seen as a large debt owing by the business to the proprietor of the company; also known as 'owner's equity'
company	a company is a business in its own right
costs	expenses incurred during the course of business
creditor	company or person to whom money is owed by the business for merchandise sold or services provided
current assets	assets which change throughout the year: for example, merchandise for sale or cash in a current bank account
current liabilities	short-term debts owed to creditors
debtor	company or person owing money to the business for merchandise sold or services provided
expenditure	outlay of money in form of expenses
expenses	costs incurred from which all benefit has been extracted during the accounting period
financial year	fiscal year – this does not automatically correspond with the Inland Revenue tax year, which runs from 1 April to 31 March; each company has its own financial year, and in the USA this frequently runs from 1 January to 31 December
fixed assets	assets which are retained for the benefit and use of the business and are not for resale
fixed liabilities	long-term debts owed by the company: for example, a mortgage or fixed term loan
investments	money invested by the business with the expectation of an increased return on capital
liabilities	debts of the business which are owed by the company
loss	the negative difference between revenue and expenses
profit	the difference between revenue and expenses

Assets and Liabilities

To understand the various financial components of a company, let us look at some of the various items that may be owned by a small factory and categorize them into assets and liabilities:

factory premises	fixed asset
material in stock	current asset
work in progress	current asset
delivery van	fixed asset
computer	fixed asset
finished merchandise	current asset
cash	current asset
building society account	investment
shares in another company	investment
mortgage	long-term liability
creditors	long-term liability
bank overdraft	short-term liability
risk capital	equity

Now that we understand more about how each item is categorized, we can look at constructing a balance sheet.

The Balance Sheet

A balance sheet can most simply be described as a snapshot of the state of a business at any given time. It is usual for companies to issue a balance sheet at the end of the accounting period, or financial year, but this does not necessarily mean that a balance sheet cannot be set up at any other time. The balance sheet is only valid for that particular date and must always have the date clearly printed at the top; it is normal practice to assume that the balance sheet information applies for the state of the business at close of business on that day.

A balance sheet does not list every single asset and liability, but gives certain information in a particular order and in a set pattern. For example, you will find that all property is listed as a fixed asset and not as individual buildings. The left-hand column lists fixed assets (property, machinery, vehicles and equipment) and current assets (merchandise in stock, work in progress, debts owing by customers and any bank account amounts). The right-hand column lists liabilities: for example, capital (owner's equity, long term loans) and current liabilities (money owing to suppliers). In the UK, you will find that a balance sheet has the assets listed on the left-hand side of the page, with the liabilities listed on the right-hand side. It may be worth noting that practices differ throughout the world: for example, in France the balance is reversed, with liabilities listed on the left and assets on the right. The whole point of a balance sheet is to ensure that the two sides balance and for this we use a simple equation:

assets = liabilities

Let us look at a very simple example of a company and the balance sheet that would be constructed at the end of its accounting period.

Example: Mr Brown's newsagency

Mr Brown owns a newsagency. He started his business with £40,000 capital and has a long-term loan from the bank for £20,000. He bought his premises for £45,000. He bought a personal computer and a cash till at a total cost of £2,000. He also bought a van for £9,000. In addition to selling newspapers, Mr Brown sells sweets, books and toys and currently has stock worth £3,000. He also has £1,000 in his current bank account. His balance sheet at the start of his business will look like Figure 27.

Mr Brown's Newsagency
Balance sheet as at 31 December 1994

FIXED ASSETS			**CAPITAL**	
Premises	45,000		Ownership interest	40,000
Van	9,000		Long-term loan	20,000
Equipment	2,000			60,000
		56,000		
CURRENT ASSETS				
Stock	3,000			
Cash in bank	1,000			
		4,000		
TOTAL ASSETS		60,000	**TOTAL LIABILITIES**	60,000

Figure 27 Mr Brown's balance sheet at the start of trading.

Mr Brown starts trading and during the first three months he buys £18,000 of stock for which he still owes £2,000. He has sold stock worth £17,000 for £29,000 but customers still owe him £1,500 for goods that they have received, but not yet paid for. His total expenses for this period have been £3,000. After his first quarter of trading, his balance sheet at the end of March would look like Figure 28.

Profit and Loss Accounts (P&L)

A profit and loss account is drawn up at the end of a fixed time to show the amount of profit or loss over this period. It is concerned only with financial performance and differs in this respect from a balance sheet, which shows financial status.

A profit and loss account therefore consists of the amount of revenue earned and the amount of expenses paid out. The difference between the two is the profit (or loss

Mr Brown's Newsagency			
Balance sheet as at 31 March 1995			
FIXED ASSETS		**CAPITAL**	
Premises	45,000	Ownership interest	40,000
Van	9,000	Long-term loan	20,000
Equipment	2,000	Profit retained*	6,000
	56,000		66,000
CURRENT ASSETS		**CURRENT LIABILITIES**	
Stock	4,000	Creditors	2,000
Debtors	1,500		
Cash in bank	6,500		2,000
	12,000		
TOTAL ASSETS	68,000	**TOTAL LIABILITIES**	68,000

These numbers are arrived at thus: stock at start of business was worth £3,000; he bought £18,000 and sold £17,000, so he has stock worth £4,000 remaining. He started with £1,000 cash in bank, and sold £29,000 worth of goods for which he has received £27,500 (still owed £1,500), giving a total of £28,500. He then paid £6,000 expenses and £16,000 for new stock, leaving him with £6,500 cash in his current account.

* Profit related to P&L becomes a liability, as it is reinvested in the business and is therefore part of capital.

Figure 28 Mr Brown's balance sheet after the first quarter of trading.

if the business is operating poorly). Therefore we can see the following equation:

revenue − expenses = profit

Revenue is taken as the amount earned through sales of merchandise and services. Expenses consist of all operating expenses, which include rents, electricity, salaries, cost of stock, etc.

Many larger companies operate with a monthly P&L which records all the revenue and expenses over the month. Within a large company the P&L will be issued by a central finance department, and it is often useful to reconcile the P&L with the department's own records to ensure that all sales records and all outgoing expenses are included to give a true view of the profit.

On a balance sheet the profit is shown as a liability and is listed on the right hand side.

Let us look again at Mr Brown's Newsagency and draw up his Profit and Loss account for the first quarter of trading (Figure 29). As you can see, the net profit is the amount of gross profit minus all expenses for this period. Net profit is carried over as capital on the balance sheet and shown as money reinvested in the business.

Simple Accounting

Purchases (£3,000 + £18,000)	21,000		Sales		29,000
Less closing stock	4,000				
Cost of goods sold		17,000			
Gross profit		12,000			
		29,000			29,000
Insurance	625		Gross profit		12,000
Wages	2,000				
Heating and lighting	375				
Rates	1,000				
General expenses	1,200				
Interest on loan	800				
		6,000			
Net profit		6,000			
		12,000			12,000

Figure 29 Example of a trading and profit and loss account.

As you can see, the net profit is the amount of gross profit minus all expenses for this period. Net profit is carried over as capital on the balance sheet and shown as money reinvested in the business.

Petty Cash

The secretary is frequently responsible for the petty cash, particularly in a smaller company. This is probably the simplest of financial records. Petty cash is used to reimburse staff for miscellaneous small sums of money: for example, cost of postage, newspapers or stationery. In some companies, travelling expenses are reimbursed via the petty cash system.

To manage the petty cash system you would require:

- a cash book in which to register all transactions (see Figure 30);
- vouchers to be completed for each transaction, to which a receipt would be attached where possible (see Figure 31);
- a lockable cash box.

The idea is that a float fixed at a certain amount and sufficient for a certain period of time (for example, £50 for a month) would be placed in the cash box. As reimbursements are made to employees, the details of each expense must be recorded on a petty cash voucher with the receipt attached. The petty cash book must then be updated with each transaction, and at the end of the month this should be balanced so that the total of the vouchers together with the remaining cash is equal to the original float. This method is known as the 'imprest' system.

You can see how important it is to record each transaction in the petty cash book together with the voucher number and the amount to ensure that the books balance

Introduction to Office Management for Secretaries

at the end of each period. The voucher is simply a record of the amount paid and the item that has been purchased. Each voucher number should be recorded in the petty cash book and the detail and amounts should also tally.

Receipts £ p	Date	Details	Voucher number	Total £ p	Postage £ p	Travel £ p	Sundries £ p
50.0	1/9/94	Cash float					
	1/9/94	Postage	1	2.13	2.13		
	3/9/94	Coffee	2	1.65			1.65
	4/9/94	Petrol – G Baxter	3	6.40		6.40	
	8/8/94	Postage	4	3.65	3.65		
	10/9/94	Postage	5	6.65	6.65		
	14/9/94	Stationery	6	2.32			2.32
	15/9/94	Postage	6	2.46	2.46		
	20/9/94	Coffee	7	1.27			1.27
	23/9/94	Petrol – L Burns	8	6.50		6.50	
	28/9/94	Postage	9	1.87	1.87		
	29/9/94	Stationery	10	3.20			3.20
				38.10	16.76	12.90	8.44
11.90	30/9/94	Cash c/d		11.90			
				50.0			

Figure 30 Example of a petty cash book.

PETTY CASH VOUCHER

Voucher No: 6   Date: 15/9/94

For what required:

	2.46
Postage	2.32
Stationery	
	4.78
Signature:	Passed by:

Figure 31 Example of a petty cash voucher.

104

Budgets

Every business has a budget for operating expenses. This is similar to a household budget, where you would make allowances for all the outgoings (for example, gas, electricity, telephone, mortgage repayments, rates, food, travel) to ensure that your monthly income is sufficient to meet these demands. You need to know how much you are likely to spend and to keep a record of this expenditure.

A business operates in the same way and often a secretary will be expected to look after a departmental budget. This simply means keeping a record of all outgoing expenditure and categorizing it in such a way that you can quickly see where money is being paid out: for example, travel, customer entertainment or stationery. You may want to include dates or other references: for example, purchase order numbers. Often you will be given an initial budget to work to. The easiest way to maintain a budget is through the use of a spreadsheet application on a computer, as this will

Budget for period 1 January to 31 March 1995			
Category	**Date**	**Amount £**	**Total £**
Hospitality events			
12 tickets to Sunset Boulevard	13 January	432	
Dinner for 12 at the Savoy	26 January	552.40	
24 tickets to the rugby international	12 February	1,248	
Opera tickets for party of 10	28 February	650	
			2,882.40
Seminars			
Product seminar	3 February	4,320	
Technical seminar	13 February	1,250	
Technical seminar	13 March	1,250	
			6,820
Public relations			
Press release	10 February	850	
Adverts × 3	11, 18, 25 Feb	7,500	
			8,350
Brochures			
500 copies of new brochure	20 February	1,500	
Designwork	16 March	2,100	
			3,600
			21,652.40
Opening budget of £25,000			25,000
Remaining budget			**3,347.60**

Figure 32 Example of a budget shown over one quarter.

allow you to add or delete entries quickly and easily while automatically updating any totals. More information on the spreadsheet facility can be found under 'Information Technology in the Office'.

Let us look at an example of a marketing department responsible for events, seminars, public relations and brochures. The initial budget for the quarter is set at £25,000 and the outgoing expenditure is grouped into the above four categories, with more detail given against each cost (see Figure 32).

Now that we have looked at the basic principles of accounting, we should look at the more mundane aspects of finance in the office: for example, expense claims, purchasing guidelines and invoice payments.

Expenses

Most companies have guidelines on what can legitimately be claimed through expense reimbursement channels. These are needed to comply with tax regulations and should therefore be adhered to.

Expense forms are usually the same throughout any company and contain certain fields which must be completed to assist the cashier in paying the claim promptly. These fields, for example, include details of expense, date, amount claimed, VAT, mileage for road travel, personnel number, department number, currency denomination (where foreign expenses may be incurred) and name. Naturally these vary between organizations, but an example is shown in Figure 33 to give you some idea of what an expenses claim form might look like.

Once claims are completed it is important to attach receipts, particularly VAT receipts, as the company can reclaim VAT in most cases (unless the company is so small that it is not VAT registered). All expenses need to be checked accurately to ensure there are no discrepancies, either in calculation or in the actual items claimed. This is needed to protect both the claimant and the authorized signatory and to ensure that audit requirements are met. The expense claim then needs to be authorized by a manager with appropriate sign-off authority, and sent to the cashier. Payment is usually made through BACS (Bank Automated Clearing System) directly to an employee's bank account.

Copies of expenses should always be kept within the department, although each employee should keep his or her own copies too. Some departments keep an expense log with details of amount and date claimed by employee. This is often used for tracking purposes or to maintain a departmental budget. Many companies issue monthly or quarterly expense records which detail all the expenses during that period for that department. Detail may be categorized by, for example, mileage rates or entertainment costs. These records may need to be reconciled against the expense vouchers received.

Name:		Date of claim:		
Personnel number:		Currency:		
Department number:		Car details:		

Date	Description	Miles	VAT	Net	Gross
	Totals				
	Less advances				
	Total claimed				

Declaration: I confirm that this claim relates to expenditure incurred wholly, necessarily and exclusively for business purposes.

Signed: _____   Date: _____

Authorized: _____   Date: _____

Figure 33 Example of an expenses claim form.

Purchasing

Most companies operate their own purchasing procedure. In larger companies there is usually a department which deals exclusively with purchasing goods and services from outside suppliers. Purchase orders are used to purchase goods or services from other companies. These forms differ from company to company but usually contain the same information fields.

Each purchase order will have its own unique number, which needs to be recorded and referred to whenever you are dealing with either the supplier or the purchasing department. In addition, there will be a field to complete for:

- the supplier's name, address, fax and telephone numbers;
- delivery address with name of contact;

- invoicing address with name of contact;
- description field to contain all relevant information on the product or service being offered, including a catalogue number or supplier's reference if appropriate;
- quantity field;
- unit price (this usually excludes VAT);
- total price (also excluding VAT);
- name and signature of person ordering;
- name and signature of authorizing person;
- department name and number (in larger organizations);
- date of order.

The top copy of this order is usually sent to the supplier, one copy is sent to the purchasing department (if there is one) and one copy is retained by the department initiating the purchase. It is useful to keep a record of all your purchase orders with some of the details that will help you to pinpoint quickly a purchase order and its current status (see Figure 34). This should be updated when the invoice is submitted and later paid.

Purchase order no.	Date sent to supplier	Supplier name	Details of purchase	Value	Date goods received	Date invoice received	Date invoice paid
C1345	15.3.95	Bloggs & Co	Stationery	£56.00	20.3.95	25.3.95	31.3.95
C1346	18.3.95	Smithson Ltd	Brochures	£364.00	20.4.95	26.4.95	8.5.95

Figure 34 Example of a purchase order log.

Payment of Invoices

Invoices are usually sent to the person responsible for ordering the product or services, although occasionally they are sent directly to a central accounting department. Most companies have specific payment terms: these may be payment within seven days, although more usually it is within 28 days of date of invoice. Invoices should be dealt with promptly to ensure swift payment. An invoice should be checked to ensure that the details are correct, that the product or service has been received and that the amount is as originally quoted. Once you are happy that the details are correct, the invoice should be authorized by the manager who originally signed the purchase order (it is helpful to add the purchase order number) and it should then be sent to the accounts payable department in a large company. This may also be known as the purchase ledger or bought ledger department.

In a smaller business, the secretary may be responsible for payment of invoices. In this case, all the details should be verified before a cheque is made out and passed to the appropriate person for signature. Details of the invoice and the cheque would then need to be entered into the purchase ledger for accounting purposes.

Business and Organization

There are many kinds of businesses, each with its own organization structure to fit the company and its goals. These fall into three main categories.

- *The public sector*: these are service companies which are owned by the state and are concerned primarily with the welfare and interests of the people, ahead of making money. They include central government departments, local authorities and councils, the civil service, police, armed forces, public corporations such as the BBC and nationalized services like the National Health Service. Many previously public companies have been privatized since 1982, including British Telecom, British Petroleum, and the electricity, gas and water companies.
- *The private sector*: these are companies which are owned by individuals (one or more) and are concerned with making profit. The private sector absorbs many organizations, including banks, insurance companies, law practices, manufacturing industries, oil industries, construction companies, retail and wholesale businesses. We will look at the private sector in some detail later in this chapter.
- *Non-profit making organizations and cooperatives*: these are companies or clubs which are established to meet a certain need. They can be charitable groups such as the NSPCC and Oxfam, or they may be professional bodies such as the CBI and the British Medical Association. Social clubs and trade unions also fall in the category of non-profit making organizations. Cooperative societies were formed in the mid-nineteenth century to ease serious unemployment. The idea was for the society to purchase goods at wholesale costs and sell to members only at market price. Profits were then divided between members in proportion to the value of their purchase – today these profits are distributed via trading stamp schemes.

The Public Sector: Structure and Control

As we have already seen, these companies were set up for the benefit of the public and are not operated for profit purposes, although they are run to break even financially. Many companies were set up by Acts of Parliament for various reasons, including:

- security – for example, police and armed services;
- fundamental importance to the country's economy;
- social necessity – for example, to provide education services or health services;
- natural monopolies – for example, British Rail (prior to its privatization).

Public corporations fall into four main categories:

- *Autonomous public corporations* which are established to perform a particular function. Such corporations have limited parliamentary involvement, but fall under the control of a particular Cabinet Minister who is responsible for presenting an Annual Report and Annual Accounts to Parliament for discussion and investigation.
- *Nationalized industries* are established to serve the public and to meet the political and economic requirements which could not be achieved efficiently through private enterprise. The principal objective is to provide a public service without making a profit, but without incurring any losses. They are fundamental to the nation's needs and cannot be allowed to fail. Various organizations were nationalized for different reasons: for example, the NHS was established to provide a health service to everyone regardless of financial status; others were nationalized to prevent an essential service falling into decline, such as British Rail; others were nationalized to provide a more efficient service, such as the Post Office.
- *Local government* bodies are responsible for all community services: for example, education, street cleaning, refuse collection, health services, drainage and maintenance of common ground. Each town or village falls under a borough which is governed by a local council. Their main areas of responsibility lie in community services, town planning, housing, police and emergency services.
- *Central government departments:* these frequently change in both roles and responsibilities according to the current government. Each department or ministry is the responsibility of a Cabinet Minister who reports directly to Parliament. Ministries include transport, education, the Foreign Office, employment, education, environment, defence, health and the Home Office among others. Each department has an annual budget for expenditure.

The Private Sector: Business Ownership

Usually a business starts as a small enterprise and grows into a larger concern, possibly becoming a multinational conglomerate. It is unusual to find a large organization mushroom overnight, but one example of this is Eurotunnel, a company formed with the specific goal of building the Channel Tunnel and in which the public were able to buy shares from the outset.

- *The sole trader*: this is the smallest kind of business, involving one person who is the sole owner of the business. He works for and controls his business. Often he will start out with a loan from the bank, but this does not mean the bank has any share in the ownership of his company. The sole trader is personally liable for all debts and claims against his business. The profit is his and not shared with others, although he may have employees working for him.

- *The partnership* is the next stage, although this may often be the starting point for a small company. In these cases, two or more people invest their capital in a business and share responsibility. The details are usually set out in a partnership deed, although this is not a legal necessity. Profits and losses are distributed among the partners and they are liable for all debts and claims against the business, both jointly and as individuals. Frequently, you will find 'sleeping partners': these are people who have invested capital in the business, but who are not involved in running it and can therefore take no part in the active business.
- *Limited liability company*: this is a company in which a number of individuals invest a certain sum of money and receive shares issued by the company. The individual's personal liability is limited to the nominal value of his shares. The assets belong to the business and not to the individuals. If one of the shareholders leaves, his shares are sold to someone else and the business continues. A limited liability company is usually set up by registration and, in accordance with the Companies Act of 1981, must have at least two shareholders. Shareholders have voting rights, with the weight of their vote dependent on the number of shares they hold, so the more shares they hold the stronger their voting right. Certain documents must be registered with the Registrar of Companies:

Memorandum of Association with details of all shareholders and the amounts of the capital they have invested. It includes a statement of the company's objectives and its main trading reasons.

Articles of Association, which detail all the internal rules of operation, the areas in which trading will take place, meeting procedures and voting rights.

Statement of Share Capital of the company for tax purposes.

Registration of directors with their names and signatures.

Registration of address for the business.

In addition, a limited liability company has to register its accounts annually with the Registrar of Companies, together with a directors' report and an annual report. A limited liability company must carry the abbreviation Ltd after its name.

- *Public limited company*: this is the term used to define a private company which has grown to such an extent that the authorized share capital exceeds £50,000. Shares can be advertised and bought publicly on the stock market. The company is then owned by the shareholders and managed by directors. It is controlled by those investors who hold a majority of shares. When a private company goes public, it becomes registered as a public limited company and must use the abbreviation plc after its name, in accordance with 1982 legislation.

As an example of a business expanding, let us once again look at Mr Brown's

Newsagency. He started his business as a sole trader with one shop and all the responsibility for the debts of his business; the profit is his and he chooses to plough it back into the business.

After two years, his shop is doing very well and Mr Brown decides he would like to expand and move into larger premises. However, this requires a lot more capital and he begins to look around for a partner to invest in his business. Mr Green has some money to invest, so the two men decide to form a partnership. They each invest £75,000 and draw up a partnership deed to this effect. They are now both liable for all claims against the business and they share the profits equally between them. They also change the name to 'Brown's & Green's Newsagency', and both take an active part in the management of the business.

After a further year, Mr Brown and Mr Green decide to take over another shop and decide it is wisest to become a limited liability company, as this will limit their own personal liability. They issue shares and two more people buy into the company. Mr Brown and Mr Green each retain 45 per cent of the shares, the two additional shareholders purchase 5 per cent each. All four shareholders have voting rights, but Mr Brown and Mr Green hold the majority. Brown's & Green's Newsagency now becomes Brown & Green Ltd.

Over the next five years, business expands and they open a further twelve newsagencies. They want to buy another newsagency chain to expand in another part of the country. The shareholders decide to float the company on the stock market, as this will give them a large amount of capital to purchase the other chain. The shares are bought by the public and the company, now known as Brown & Green plc as it is now a public limited company, has 36 shops and is managed by a board of directors of which Mr Brown is the chairman.

This simple example gives you an idea of how a business can expand from a small corner shop to a nationwide public company.

Organization Structure

Companies are established to fulfil certain goals: for example, the production and sale of goods or services. This involves a succession of activities which in turn develop into an organizational structure in which each employee has his own tasks, duties and responsibilities. This organizational structure must be appropriate for the business goals and must have a central authority. As companies grow, their status changes in many ways.

Many organizational structures are developed haphazardly as the company grows. For example, a sole trader will do everything for himself: this will include purchasing his stock, selling his stock and keeping his own accounts. As the company grows he will employ people to take on certain roles and gradually an organizational infrastructure forms. In most corporate businesses, the organization structure is firmly in place and very similar to others in the industry in which the enterprise operates. We will look at various organization structures, together with the different functions and their principal roles and responsibilities.

All limited companies have a certain conforming hierarchical structure which enables clear lines of responsibility and reporting requirements. Figure 35 depicts the organization of a private limited company and the various roles involved.

```
                        SHAREHOLDERS
                             |
                     BOARD OF DIRECTORS
                             |
                             |———————— COMPANY SECRETARY
              ┌──────────────┴──────────────┐
         CHAIRMAN                    CHIEF EXECUTIVE or
                                     MANAGING DIRECTOR
              └──────────────┬──────────────┘
                             |
                     EXECUTIVE DIRECTORS
```

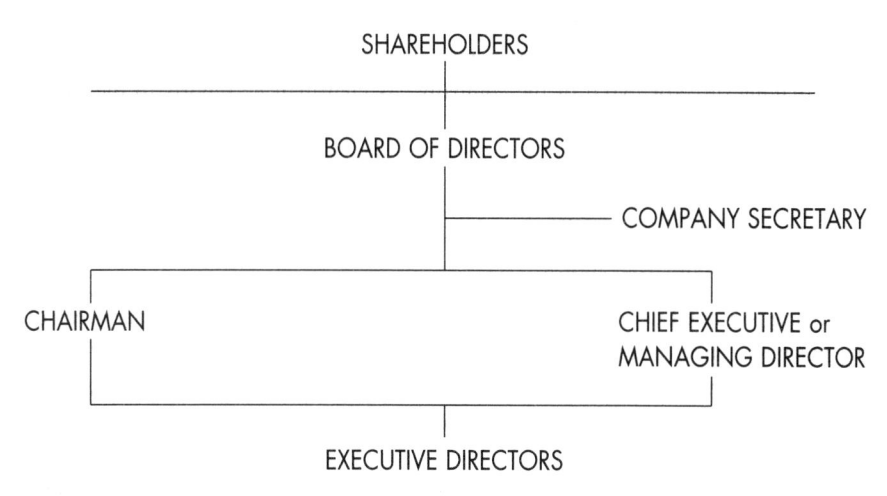

Figure 35 Example of the hierarchical structure of an organization.

Roles and Responsibilities

- *The shareholders* own 'shares' or stocks in the company and have some voting rights in the running of the company. In many corporations the employees may hold stock in the company in which they work. These shares are frequently purchased through a special stock purchase plan which offers some incentive to employees to purchase shares: for example, the shares may be offered at a discounted price. In these cases, the shareholders are involved in the company and should therefore have a greater interest in the profits of the business.
- *The board of directors* is a body of people who are responsible for making general policy decisions and determining what happens to the company's profits. The board is elected annually by the shareholders, although there are often no changes in the members from one year to the next. They meet regularly as a group and are composed of both company employees and external advisers. The board members can be divided into 'executive directors' who actually work in the company and 'non-executive directors' who do not work in the company, but who bring a certain knowledge or experience. Frequently, directors are specialists in their own particular area and will often hold places on a number of boards. Many MPs sit on company boards. In a family business it is usual to find family members on the board, who may or may not work for the company.

Introduction to Office Management for Secretaries

- *The company secretary* holds an administrative and advisory position, reporting to the board. Frequently this role may be combined with that of the company's legal adviser, who has the added responsibility of legal counsel to the company, or it could be combined with the position of chief accountant. The company secretary is responsible for the administration of the board matters: for example, setting up the meetings, distributing the agenda and taking the minutes.
- *The chairman* is often the same person as the chief executive officer (CEO) or managing director (MD) of the company. As chairman he reports to the shareholders and is accountable for the overall business: for example, its financial status and policies.
- *The chief executive officer* may also be known as the managing director and is responsible to the board of directors for the general running of the business and for its continued financial status.

Reporting to the CEO are the executive directors responsible for particular areas of the business. They, in turn, will have a number of directors or managers with responsibility for various areas reporting to them. In general, the larger an organization, the more complex the structure, with more levels of management between the office worker and the CEO.

A typical organization will have a structure with around six or seven main functions which may fall into several categories, according to the nature of the industry in which the company is operating. Figure 36 shows one example.

Naturally, organization structures will vary from one company to the next and that in Figure 36 is just an example of the sort of infrastructure you may find in a large company that is selling products or services to its customers. Depending on the nature of the business, you may find a manufacturing director or other directors. Many departments may have different reporting channels according to the different companies: for example, in Figure 36 information technology reports to administration, but in many companies it reports to the finance director, and in an IT-intensive company you may find an information technology director. The organization chart for a bank or a law practice would be very different.

Let us look at the main functions of the organization and their different roles and responsibilities in more detail.

Sales

The sales director is responsible for the entire salesforce. Depending upon the product or service that is being sold, a salesforce may be organized on a geographical or industry base. For example, a salesman selling promotional gifts may have all the companies in South East London as his territory, and would therefore have a geographical base, or he may have all the companies in the transport sector, which means he would be industry based. In either event, there will be a sales manager who is re-

Business and Organization

```
                        ┌──────────────────────┐
                        │ Chief executive officer │
                        └──────────────────────┘
```

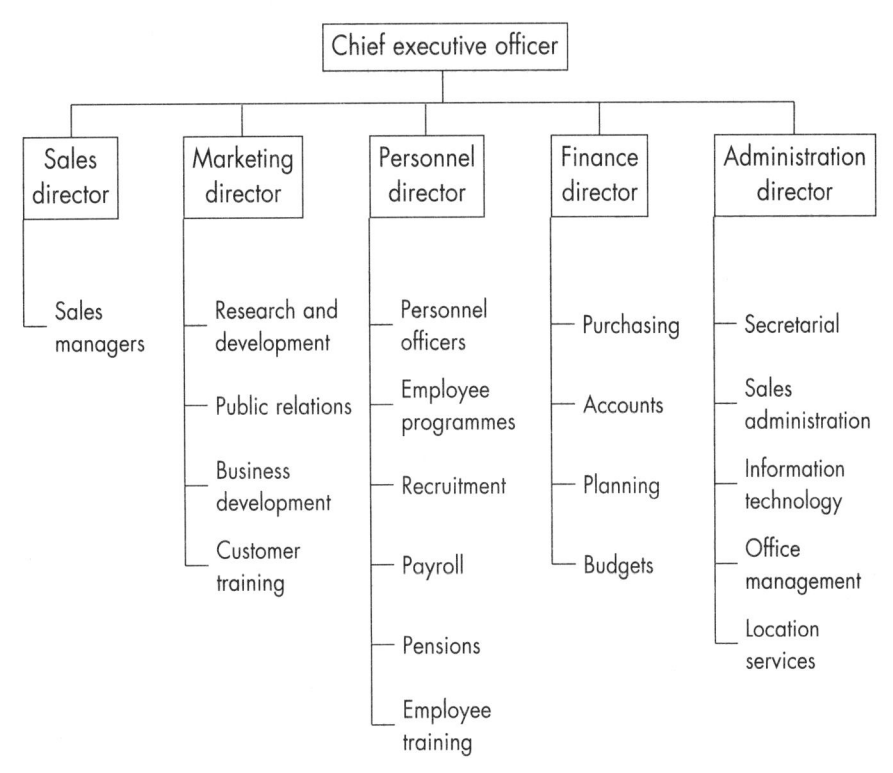

Sales director	Marketing director	Personnel director	Finance director	Administration director
Sales managers	Research and development	Personnel officers	Purchasing	Secretarial
	Public relations	Employee programmes	Accounts	Sales administration
	Business development	Recruitment	Planning	Information technology
	Customer training	Payroll	Budgets	Office management
		Pensions		Location services
		Employee training		

Figure 36 Example of an organizational chart.

sponsible for the sales people in his area. The sales director will hold regular sales meetings to enable him to measure their progress against targets and to update his salesforce on various matters which may affect them.

At the beginning of each financial year, a company will have certain targets it will want, or need, to achieve. These are generally based on revenue or profit targets. It is the sales director's responsibility to analyse these targets based on past and current performance, and to forecast which areas are likely to achieve higher success rates and which will be more difficult. With this in mind, he will allocate targets to his sales managers, who will pass them on to his sales people.

So at the beginning of each year, each sales representative will have a target which he needs to achieve. This is usually measured on a monthly, quarterly or annual basis, with commission being paid at the same intervals. The sales representative will look at his accounts in detail and will forecast his own figures. It is then up to him to decide how he wants to go about achieving his targets and to implement his plan.

The sales director and sales managers are there to provide direction, assistance and motivation to their salesforce. Frequently they will actively participate in the key accounts or in difficult situations where the presence of a more senior employee will help close a sale.

To do their job effectively, the salesforce need to be kept aware of the product range, forthcoming products and any promotional offers that may help them to achieve their sales. In this respect they work very closely with the various departments reporting to the marketing director.

Marketing

The marketing director has overall responsibility for marketing the product from the early steps of research and development to the latter stage of promotion and advertising. This activity involves certain elements:

- determining the market place;
- research and development;
- cost of manufacturing and distribution;
- pricing policy;
- advertising and promotion;
- monitoring and keeping up to date with competitors' products, prices and promotions;
- communications.

Let us look at the various departments you will find reporting to the marketing director and the functions they perform in the overall scheme of marketing a product.

Research and development

This department will look at the various factors which determine the position of a product in the market place: for example, for a new product they will investigate the size of the market, other similar products already on sale, competition and pricing. With a current product they may look at extending a product line and will consider enhancements to the original design and previous sales success. When examining the market place they will consider the following factors, which influence the selling ability of a product:

- warranty and after-care service;
- reputation of the company and the product;
- need/demand;
- quality standard;
- presentation of product;
- compatibility with other products;
- performance (particularly important in comparison with competitors' products);
- ease of use.

Once a product has been manufactured and is ready for sale, they will look at the pricing policy. The price of a product depends on various ingredients. For example:

- expenditure on materials, manpower, production overheads (including heating, lighting, machinery);
- cost of production;
- cost of marketing and selling;
- comparison with similar products on sale by competitors;
- demand for the product;
- profit.

Once these various elements have been taken into account, a price will be fixed. The next responsibility for the research and development department is to monitor how the product is sold and its position in the market place.

Public relations

The public relations (PR) department's role is to use various advertising and press media to promote the product to encourage sales. This is done through the following.

- *Advertising campaigns*: here there is a variety of media and the choice is usually dependent on cost and the target market place. Newspapers, both national and local, and magazines, particularly special interest or trade magazines, are a popular choice. A more expensive, but very effective medium, is television (and, to a lesser extent, radio), as this reaches a far wider audience. Other advertising methods include billboards and posters on public transport. The purpose of advertising is to promote a product and to show it to advantage against a similar product from a competitor. The main disadvantage is the cost, which in turn increases the cost of the product to the consumer.
- *Product launches*: at which a particular product is 'unveiled' to a select audience of prospective purchasers and is usually accompanied by a key speaker and refreshments to encourage people to attend and view the product. Frequently journalists are present at this sort of event and free publicity is generated as a result.

It is also the PR department's responsibility to deal with any questions relating to the company and any aspect of its performance or product range. The PR department is the link between the business and the press, which must be handled with care as the press hold a lot of responsibility for the making or the breaking of a product, or a company.

Business development

This is becoming a key role in most large organizations. The purpose of a business development department is to conduct research into the market place and to analyse the findings, with a view to getting a better idea of the company's position in the market place. This research can be extremely valuable in identifying opportunities in the market place based on current trends. Additionally, an awareness of competitors, together with their products, prices and promotion campaigns, can assist a company in making decisions about its own marketing policy. Business development is all about looking for opportunities and promoting these opportunities in the best possible way to gain maximum benefit for the company. In addition to conducting research, the business development department is frequently responsible for organizing seminars and events to promote products and services. This may take the form of technical seminars to demonstrate a product, or hospitality events to encourage a good working relationship between the salesman and his client.

Customer training

Many businesses will sell products or services to their clients which require training. For example, a computer company selling a particular package might offer training to the customer on how to use the package. This customer training is an extension of the product in so far as it is important to establish the right image and provide a professional service to the customer. The training department's role is to set up training courses which meet the demands of its customers in terms of content, length and cost. It needs to coordinate the courses and advertise them.

Personnel

The personnel director is responsible for all aspects of employee programmes, from the recruitment of new staff to the time they leave the company and their pension requirements. Personnel is divided into several departments, which focus on different aspects.

Personnel officers

In most large companies, there are personnel officers whose role is to 'look after' the employee. This is frequently an advisory and counselling position, as the personnel officers' primary concern is the welfare of the employee and they are there to give advice to both employees and employers on any personnel related matter: for example, holidays, sickness pay, disciplinary matters and job changes. Frequently they are also involved in recruitment and redundancy schemes.

Employee programmes

This department is responsible for any employee benefits: for example, company cars, health insurance, life assurance, maternity benefits and house moves. Departmental staff must ensure that they are kept up to date with what other companies of a similar nature are doing. The department is responsible for all the administration involved in running these programmes.

Recruitment

This department's role is to deal with all aspects of recruitment:

- advertising job vacancies internally and externally;
- receiving and sifting through CVs and applications;
- responding to candidates as appropriate;
- setting up interviews and running recruitment days;
- ensuring correct procedures are met;
- issuing offer or rejection letters.

Payroll

The payroll department is responsible for maintaining all salary records and registering any changes that may affect an employee's salary: for example, promotion, holiday or sickness. The payroll department ensures that the payroll run is effected and that employees are given the appropriate payslips. It is responsible for all aspects of National Insurance, tax and pension deductions and will be able to advise the employee on any such issues.

Pensions

The pensions department is responsible for all administration of employees' pensions. This involves issuing details of the company pension plan (if appropriate), advising on an employee's salary deduction for pension purposes, administering the pension of those employees who have retired from the company and dealing with any queries on pensions that the employee may have.

Employee training

Many companies provide training for their employees. This may be done in-house or through an external supplier. The training department will offer a schedule of the available courses, advise on the suitability of a course for an employee, enrol students on courses and send out information. Many larger companies offer training on business and personal skills, technical skills and management development, although naturally the selection of courses will vary from one company to the next.

Finance

The finance director is responsible for all aspects of finance and planning for the company. This involves many duties and these are often divided into the following departments.

Purchasing is responsible for purchasing goods or services from external suppliers at the best possible price. In a large company, the purchasing department will negotiate prices and may establish contracts with certain suppliers, which will achieve cost savings. The larger the company, the greater the purchasing power, as suppliers are keen to have regular orders from large companies. An example of this could be the cost of hotel accommodation charged to a large company: rooms are offered at a cost around 30 per cent lower than that paid by the average customer. This cost is offset against the number of hotel nights which a company is likely to provide over a certain period, which enables the hotel to provide accommodation at a more competitive price.

Accounts deals with all the accounts and invoices for goods and services purchased or sold by the company. This may be divided into two departments:

- *Accounts payable* (sometimes known as bought ledger or purchase ledger) is responsible for payment and recording of all invoices for goods or services purchased. Invoices must be checked to ensure that the goods have been received and approved before a cheque is raised, signed and sent to the supplier within the required payment terms.
- *Sales ledger* is responsible for sending out invoices for goods or services sold to customers and for ensuring payment is made to the company.

Business and financial planning: usually business planning is done on a three to five year basis, with the aim of forecasting any future business activity and economic changes which may affect the revenue and profit of a company. This is in turn incorporated into a business plan which sets out certain objectives for the company to achieve its goals. For example, the recruitment activity and headcount plan is a key aspect of any business plan, and aims to ensure that adequate resources are available to meet demands on the business or, in a declining economy, that redundancy packages are targeted. Planning is an essential ingredient in the success or failure of a company.

Budgets: various factors need to be examined to determine the amount of budget available for expenditure and the allocation of budgets to departments. This department is responsible for ensuring that budgets are correctly managed and that expenses are allocated to the correct budgets.

Administration

The administration director is responsible for all aspects of administration within the company. This department is frequently combined with finance as the two areas often overlap. In addition to the areas already looked at in finance, the administration director will be responsible for the following.

Secretarial staff: ensuring that each department has the correct number of secretaries with the appropriate skills to support the business. Frequently Youth

Trainees may be employed to assist secretaries and to achieve some administrative experience in the workplace to enable them to move into a secretarial career after their courses have been completed. In these cases, a Youth Trainee supervisor will be appointed who will offer the Youth Trainees help and advice with their course material and work experience

Sales administration: this is a very important area as the sales administrators are responsible for all aspects of a customer order once the salesman has signed the contract. Their role is to process the order, which may involve checking all the details of the contract before entering it into the order entry system, advising the shipping department as to which products to send, together with the client's details and address, and informing the sales ledger department of all details needed to send out the invoice. It is important to remember that every company has its own processes and ways of performing duties, and this is one area in which every company is different.

Information technology: this department is responsible for looking at the IT requirements of each department and fulfilling these requirements with the most appropriate hardware equipment and software packages. In addition to purchasing, it will be responsible for installing and maintaining the equipment, which may involve the installation of networks or other cabling out of business hours to cause minimum disruption. The IT department also provides a 'help desk' facility to assist with any problems or queries on the equipment that is being used. Frequently the department will arrange training for any new products.

Office management: office managers are responsible for the office environment. Their duties include, for example:

- ensuring adequate supplies of stationery are available;
- keeping supplies of fuses, light bulbs, plugs and other miscellaneous items which may be needed;
- liaising with cleaners to ensure a clean and safe office environment;
- allocating desk space, cupboards and equipment to employees;
- arranging for the repair and maintenance of equipment like photocopiers.

There are many duties for the office manager, but these vary greatly from one company to the next.

Location services: this department may fall under the responsibility of the Office Manager, but will include services which are used by all employees, such as:

- mailing facilities and post room;
- repair and maintenance of equipment;
- lighting and heating;
- switchboard equipment and staff;
- reception area and receptionist staff.

Appendix 1: Useful Telephone Numbers

Railway Telephone Information Services

Network South Central Ltd	01273 324487
South Eastern Train Co Ltd	0345 484950
LTS Rail Ltd	0171-620 5760
Chiltern Railways Co. Ltd	0171-922 9522
North London Railways Ltd	01923 207818
Great Northern Railway Ltd	0345 226688
Thameslink Rail Ltd	0171-329 4106
Great Eastern Railway Ltd	0171-247 5488

Rail enquiries for London area

North East and South London	0345 484950
South Midlands and West London	0345 484950
North West London	0345 484950
North London	0345 484950

Other services

International rail travel	0171-834 2345
British Rail International Ltd (Europe)	0171-834 2345
Passenger liaison	0171-620 5555
Group travel	0171-626 1671
Lost property enquiries	0171-928 5151
Red Star Parcels Ltd	0345 000000
Sleeper reservations for	
North West England and Scotland	0171-388 6061
West of England	0171-313 1950
Credit card bookings	
InterCity West	0171-387 8541

Network SouthCentral Ltd   0345 484950
South Eastern Train Co Ltd   0345 484950
Thameslink Rail Ltd   0345 484950

World Airlines Telephone Information Services

Aer Lingus   01645 737747
Air Canada   0800 181313
Air France   0181-742 6600
Air India   0171-491 7979
Air UK   0345 666777
Alitalia   0171-602 7111
American Airlines   0181-572 5555
British Airways   0181-897 4000
British Midland   0171-589 5599
Cathay Pacific   0171-747 8888
Iberia   0171-437 5622
Japan Airlines   0171-408 1000
KLM   0181-750 9000
Lufthansa   0345 737747
Qantas   0345 747767
Sabena   0181-780 1444
SAS   0171-734 4020
Swissair   0171-439 4144
TWA   0171-439 0707
Virgin Atlantic   01293 562000

Regional Airport Telephone Numbers

Aberdeen   01224 722331
Belfast International   01849 422999
Birmingham   0121-767 5511
Bournemouth   01202 593939
Bristol   01179 874441
Cardiff   01446 711111
Coventry   01203 301717
East Midlands   01332 810621
Edinburgh   0131-333 1000
Glasgow   0141-887 1111

Appendix 1

Humberside	01652 688456
Leeds Bradford	01132 509696
London City	0171-474 5555
London Gatwick	01293 535353
London Heathrow	0181-759 4321
Luton	01582 405100
Stansted	01279 680500
Teesside	01325 332811
Manchester	0161-489 3000
Newcastle	0191-286 0966
Southampton	01703 629600

UK Hotel Group Telephone Information Services

Forte Group	0345 404040
Forte Posthouse	0800 404040
Forte Travelodge	0800 850950
Hilton National	0171-734 6000
Hilton International	0345 581595
Intercontinental	0181-847 2277
Jarvis Hotels	0345 581237
Whitbread Travel Inn	01582 482224

Car Hire Companies: Central Reservation Numbers

Avis	0181-848 8733
Budget	0800 181181
Europcar	0181-950 5050
Eurodollar	01895 33300
Hertz	0181-679 1799
Automobile Association Breakdowns	0345 887766

Other Useful Numbers

London Transport	0171-222 1234
Motorail Services	0345 090700

Useful Telephone Numbers

Eurostar	0345 881881
Le Shuttle	0990-700800
P&O European Services	01304 203388
Stena Sealink	01233 647047
Sally Line	01843 595522

Appendix 2: Secretarial Survey

The Survey

A survey was carried out of a selection of the top fifty UK companies, financial institutions, secretarial colleges and recruitment agencies. The aim of the survey was to discover the most sought after skills in the recruitment of secretaries.

I would like to thank the following companies for their valuable input, particularly for the many useful comments and feedback I received. My acknowledgements also go to those companies who responded, but did not wish to be mentioned by name.

Alfred Marks
Allied Lyons plc
Argyll Group plc
Asda Group plc
Bass plc
British Steel plc
British Aerospace
British Gas plc
British Petroleum plc
British Airways plc
Broadway Secretarial Training
BTR plc
Citibank NA
Eagle Star Insurance
ECCO Employment
Engelhard Ltd
First Direct
Ford Motor Company plc
Gallaher Ltd
GEC Ltd
Halifax Building Society
Hampstead Secretarial College
Hanson plc

Harrow Secretarial College
IBM (UK) Ltd
Imperial Chemical Industries plc
Institut Français du Royaume-Uni
J Sainsbury plc
Lloyds Bank plc
Lucy Clayton Secretarial College
Manpower
Nationwide Anglia
Norwich Union
Oracle (UK) Ltd
Pensinsular & Oriental Steam Navigation Company
Prudential Corporation plc
Queens' Secretarial College
Reed Employment
Rolls Royce plc
Royal Dutch/Shell Group
St James' Secretarial College
The Post Office
Thorn EMI plc
Unilever plc

The survey was divided into business and personal skills, which companies were asked to rank by importance.

Results

It was interesting to discover that personal skills achieved higher results than business skills, showing that companies are now seeking secretaries of a different calibre who can combine their personal skills with their business proficiency.

Below the results are given in order of priority, with number one being the most sought after business skill/personal skill:

Business skills

1. Computer/word processing knowledge.
2. Good English grammar and spelling.
3. Telephone techniques.
4. Typing/shorthand/audio skills.
5. Organization ability.
6. Diary and meeting management.
7. Handling correspondence.

Appendix 2

8 Past experience and track record.
9 Company/market knowledge.
10 Foreign languages.

Personal skills

1 Positive attitude.
2 Flexibility.
3 Efficiency and good organization.
4 Personality and disposition.
5 Communication and speech techniques.
6 Self-motivation.
7 Good time management.
8 Smart appearance.
9 Confidence in own ability.
10 Innovation and creativity.

Index

A

accounting terms 98
accounts 99, 100, 120–1
action file 27
activity log 18–19
administration 42, 120–1
advertising 117
agenda 69, 70
Allen, Fred 66
answerphones 47
appearance 15–17
arithmetic logic unit 80
Articles of Association 111
Ash, Mary Kay 17
assets 99, 100, 101, 102
attitude 5, 15, 16–17, 30, 36

B

Babbage, Charles 77
BACS (Bank Automated Clearing System) 106
back–up 84, 85
badge card reader 81
balance sheet 100, 101, 102
Barco 70, 82
batch processing 97
behaviour 3, 5, 6, 17, 36
Bliss, Edwin 24
board of directors 112, 113
body language 3, 5–14
bookkeeping 98
bought ledger 98
bring forward files/system 23, 56
BSI (British Standards Institute) 37
budget(s) 98, 105–6, 120
Burton, Robert 26
business development 117–18

C

calendar 25, 95
capital 99, 101
cash book 103
chairman 41, 112, 114
checklist 26, 27, 34
chief executive 114
clock 101
clothing 15
comfort zones 6–7
communication
  electronic 88–90
  telephone 44–7
  verbal 3, 4, 35
  written 35, 48
compact disk (CD) 85
company secretary 114
complaints 46
computer 69, 76, 77, 89, 90–1, 118
Computer Misuse Act 90–1
conferences 68
control unit 80, 83
co-operatives 109
correspondence 18, 54, 59
costs 99
CPU (central processing unit) 78, 79, 80, 84, 97
creditor 99
customer 36, 37, 46, 56, 58, 59, 61, 118
customer care 35–6

Index

D

daisy wheel printer 83
Data Protection Act 91
databases 94–5
day book 27
deadlines 18, 20, 21, 24, 25, 42, 57
debtor 99
departments 40, 433
desk 22–3
desktop 67
desktop publishing 96
diaries 18, 29, 61
diary management 61
disk drive 79, 83
diskette(s) 23, 85, 86, 89
disk(s) 78, 84–5
DOS (disk operating system) 91, 92, 97
Dos Passos, John 22
dot matrix printers 83
double-entry book keeping 98
dress 15–16

E

electronic mail 44, 88–9, 90
electronic office 61, 76, 88–9
employee 57, 59, 118, 119
environment (working) 18, 22, 30
equity 100
events 59, 61, 66, 72–5, 105, 118
expenditure 98, 99, 105, 110
expense(s) 98, 99, 101, 102, 103, 106
eyes 14

F

facsimile 47–8
feed
    continuous 84
    sheet 84
    tractor 84
file server 86, 88
filing 20, 27, 55, 59, 94

finance 99, 115, 119–20
financial year 99, 100, 115
Franklin, Benjamin 63

G

general ledger 98
government
    central 110
    local 110
graphics 93, 96
GUI (graphic user interface) 92, 97
guidelines 41, 44, 75, 105

H

hands 8–10, 13
hard disk 83, 84
hardware 91
head positions 10–11
Hollerith, Hermann 77
Honey, Peter 17

I

icon 92
impact printers 82
Imprest system 98
influence 1
information technology 76, 121
inkjet printers 83–4
input devices 79, 80–1
Internet 88, 90
in-tray 23
investment 99, 100
invoices 109, 120
ISO (International Standards Organization) 37

J

Jacquard, Joseph Marie 77

K

keyboard 79, 80, 83
Kissinger, Henry 62

130

Index

L

LAN (local area network) 86, 87, 88, 97
laptop(s) 28, 77, 78
laser printers 84
layout 49–53, 96
leavers 27
ledger 98
liabilities 99, 100, 101
limited liability company 111, 112
line printer 83
listening 3, 32, 45
lists 18–20
location services 121
log 18–20, 49, 56, 108
loss 99

M

mail 18, 48, 49, 55, 56
mainframe 77
Malby, Jack 54
management (self) 18
manager 13, 39–40, 58, 61
marketing 105, 116
meeting(s) 18, 29, 59, 62, 66, 68, 71
Memorandum of Association 111
memory unit 78, 80
Meskiman, John 21
message 74
  taking 44, 45
  voicemail 47
micro computers 78
microfiche 82
microfilm 82
mini computers 78
minutes
  layout 71
  taking 71–2
mobile telephones 28, 74
mouse 81, 83
multi-tasking 97

N

network(s) 86, 88, 89
new starters 27, 118
Newton, Howard 17
nominal ledger 98
non-impact printers 82
notebook(s) 2, 62, 77, 78, 82

O

objectives 31
OCR (optical character recognition) 81
off-line 97
online 97
operating system 79–80, 91, 92
optical
  card reader 81
  wand 81
organization 24, 113–14
organization chart 24, 26, 28
organizing events 66
output devices 79, 82

P

P&L (profit and loss) 101–2
pagers 28
partnership 111, 112
Pascal, Blaise 77
password 90
payroll 119
pecking order 21
pen 81
pending file 27
pensions 110
perception awareness 1–2, 44
personal computer (PC) 22, 68, 77–9, 83, 84
personal organizers 29
personnel 118
petty cash 98, 103–4
planning 22, 32, 62, 74, 119, 120
Plato 32
plotter 83

Index

positive thinking 17
presentations 29, 34, 35, 69, 70, 74, 95–6
pressure 9, 21, 22, 37
printer(s) 79, 82–4
prioritizing 21
private sector 109–11
professionalism 17, 29, 37
profit 60, 99, 101, 102, 112
project team 40
projects 30, 31, 34
promotional events 73, 74
public limited company 111
public relations 105, 117
public sector 109–10
punchcards 77, 81
purchase ledger 98, 109
purchase order 106–8
purchasing 107, 108, 120

Q

quality 37, 38, 116

R

Rayburn, Sam 4
real-time 68, 97
reception 121
record(s) 18, 57, 58, 89, 94, 103, 105, 108
recruitment 118, 119
references 48–9
relationships 39, 42
reports 31, 34, 60
reputation 36
requirements 31, 32, 33
research and development 116–17
Roosevelt, Franklin 18
RSI (repetitive strain injury) 22
Rusk, Dean 4

S

sales 114–16, 121
sales ledger 98, 120

secretarial bible 26
secretarial team 42–3
security 89
shareholders 111, 112, 113
signature book 58
softcopy 61
software 88, 89, 91
sole trader 110–11, 112
spreadsheets 93–4, 105
starters 27, 118
stationery 23, 28
storage 78, 79, 84
switchboard 121
Syrus, Publius 15

T

tape 85
team(s) 39, 43
technology 76, 77
teleconferencing 44, 66
telephone 3, 4, 18, 23, 24, 36, 44, 45, 66, 74, 116
terminal 22, 86
terminology 97
terms of reference 30, 31, 34–5
thermal printer 83
time management 18
to do list 20
tone 3, 4, 5
touch sensitive screen 81
training 118, 119
travel 29, 63–5, 105

U

useful numbers 24

V

VDU (visual display unit) 82, 97
verbal communication 3, 4. 35
video conferencing 44, 66–8
   desktop 67
   rollabout 67
   studio 67

video output 82
viruses 90, 91
voice input 81
voice output 82
voicemail 44, 47

W

WAN (wide area network) 86, 87, 88, 97
Windows 68, 91, 92, 96
word processing 91, 95, 96

working environment 18, 22, 30
working relationships 43
workload 21
workplan 24, 25
written communication 35, 48–53

Z

zone 6, 7, 14